ALISTAIR BEGG

The
HAND
of
GOD

Finding His Care
in All Circumstances

Scripture quotations, unless noted otherwise, are taken from the *Holy Bible: New International Version*®. NIV®. Copyright © 1973, 1978, 1984, International Bible Society. Used by permission of Zondervan Publishing House. All rights reserved.

The "NIV" and "New International Version" trademarks are registered in the United States Patent and Trademark Office by International Bible Society. Use of either trademark requires permission of International Bible Society.

ISBN: 0-8024-1704-3

3 5 7 9 10 8 6 4 2

Printed in the United States of America

The
HAND
of
GOD

To Derek J. Prime,
With admiration and affection

ACKNOWLEDGMENTS

Every writing project is a team effort. Every member of the team is important and deserving of recognition. Once again, as before, I've been humbled to be on the receiving end of the gentle proddings and genuine encouragements which have been provided consistently by Greg Thornton, Jim Bell, Bill Thrasher, and Bill Soderberg. To be supported by this gang of four from Moody Press means more than I can adequately convey. As always, I'm in the debt of my secretary, Kay Roberts, who has managed so many of the details from the inception to the conclusion of the project. On this occasion in the final stages, I was also greatly helped by Jeanne Bernier, to whom I owe a debt of gratitude. Both of these ladies represent the wide circle of support which surrounds me here at Parkside Church. To the elders and congregation who pray regularly for me, I express my deepest thanks.

One individual in particular deserves special mention, namely Phil Rawley, without whom this book would literally never have seen the light of day. His thumbprint appears on every page and it has been a genuine privilege for me to work with Phil on this most import of projects.

I acknowledge again my deepest gratitude to my wife, Susan, and to each of my children, who are always keen to see the finished product, having been such a part of its formation.

Finally I gladly acknowledge my gratitude to parents, Sunday school teachers, Bible class leaders, and pastors who have over the years taught me the great stories of the Bible and stirred my heart with a love for the lessons of God's Word, one of which is contained in the pages that follow.

CONTENTS

FAMILY TIES

We know that in all things God works for the good of those who love him, who have been called according to his purpose."

Those who have been Christians for any length of time, may find that the page in their Bible which contains Romans 8:28 may be a little worn, even smudged. And with good reason. This great verse is a promise from God that we are not hapless victims of life, at the mercy of fate or chance. We are not driven along by some blind, impersonal force.

On the contrary, we are the objects of God's providential care. We are under His guiding and protecting hand.

The providence of God is "that continued exercise of the divine energy whereby the creator preserves all his creatures, is operative in all that comes to pass in the world, and directs all things to their appointed end" (Berkhof).

The implications of this truth are staggering because they impact every area and every moment of our lives. This truth is one of the things that separates believers from unbelievers. We need not be concerned about Sagittarius or Gemini or the other signs of the zodiac, or about the movements of the planets and other silly things that preoccupy pagan minds. Jesus says they may run after these things (Matthew 6:32), but as His people we are to be different.

So we are faced with this incredible truth that God rules and overrules in all the circumstances of life. Romans 8:28 is not a pious platitude to be mumbled at a bedside or a graveside when we don't know what else to say but want to be helpful. It is truth that's meant for life, so what we need is a real-life illustration of how this truth looks "with skin on."

That's what we hope to discover in this book. This biblical doctrine is classically expressed in the story of Joseph. As we trace the powerful principle of God's providential care unfolding in the life of the patriarch Joseph, we will find that his story is probably *the* classic Old Testament illustration of Romans 8:28 in action.

If you enjoy stories as much as I do, I can assure you that we are at the threshold of a classic in the story of Joseph. Indeed, it is an epic, a saga. The biography of Joseph covers more space than that given to any of the other heroes in the book of Genesis. That's amazing when you realize that this group includes Abraham, the friend of God and the father of all who believe.

Even people who have only a scant knowledge of the Old Testament probably know of Joseph for the same reason many people know of Noah and the ark or Jonah and the great fish. His story is memorialized by something visually unusual—his multicolored coat.

And for those who have no biblical clue at all, Joseph may still be a familiar name, courtesy of the popular Broadway musical *Joseph and the Amazing Technicolor Dreamcoat*, by Timothy Rice and Andrew Lloyd-Weber. Joseph, as we are about to discover, is a man worth knowing.

Joseph's birth is recorded in Genesis 30:23–24, and he is mentioned several times in subsequent chapters. But we are introduced to him in depth when he is seventeen years old, a young man tending the flocks of his father, Jacob, with his brothers (Genesis 37:2). Between this notice and the record of Joseph's death ninety-three years later at the age of 110 (50:26), we have the details of a truly amazing life presented to us in biblical Technicolor.

The story of Joseph is a tale of jealousy, deceit, slavery,

misrepresentation, injustice, lust, rivalry, and forgiveness. It pits brother against brother. We encounter imprisonment and deep trials that do not produce self-pity, and prosperity that does not bring the accompanying pride.

Joseph's life encompasses all of this and more. And in it all the overarching theme is that of the sovereign hand of God manifesting itself in His providential care over His dearly loved children and bringing about all that He has purposed in the affairs of time.

Joseph's life ought to be for us a story of great encouragement and reassurance as we make our way in the walk of faith, carrying with us the baggage of our past, the fears of our present, and the prospects of our future. We are sometimes tempted to wonder in the midst of all the pieces of the jigsaw puzzle of life, *Does God care? Is God in control? And if so, what might we expect?*

We don't know if Joseph asked those questions before he was seventeen. We will see that his early life did include a great amount of turmoil, in large part because his father, Jacob's, past was catching up with him.

But if Joseph never had reason to wonder what God was doing in his life, all of that changed when he turned seventeen. Before we look at the events that sent Joseph's life spinning, let's consider the influences on his life up to that point.

JOSEPH'S BACKGROUND

Where did Joseph come from? If you were to encounter his name for the first time in Genesis 37:2, you might ask this. Did Joseph have the kind of family background we might expect to produce a person of such exceptional character?

What were Joseph's family ties? All of us have them, and they all mean something. Our family ties can be frustrating and full, blessed and benighted.

There's no question that Joseph came from quite a family. No other seventeen-year-old can boast that his great-grandfather is Abraham; his grandfather, Isaac; and his father, Jacob.

By looking at Jacob we can trace the family ties and the influences of Joseph's early life.

Jacob's Early Life

Jacob's character was revealed at his birth when he grasped the heel of his twin Esau and was given a name that means "deceiver" or "chiseler" (see Genesis 25:26, margin). Jacob was aptly named for he was skillful at manipulating people and events to get things to turn out the way he wanted. The first thing we learn about him is that he chiseled his elder brother, Esau, out of his birthright (vv. 27–34).

Then, as recorded in Genesis 27, Jacob deceived his father Isaac into conferring upon him the blessing that should have belonged to Esau. When Esau found out, he said, "Isn't he rightly named Jacob? He has deceived me these two times" (27:36). Esau vowed to kill Jacob, so his mother Rebekah sent Jacob to live with her brother Laban in the land of Paddan Aram (28:2).

It was there that Jacob met and fell in love with Rachel, the younger daughter of Laban (29:9–10, 16–18). Jacob loved Rachel so passionately he offered to work for his Uncle Laban seven years for Rachel's hand in marriage.

Now, ironically, Uncle Laban was a bit of a schemer himself. So when the seven years were completed and Jacob said to Laban, "Give me my wife. My time is completed, and I want to lie with her" (v. 21), Laban deceived Jacob by slipping his older daughter Leah into the wedding chamber.

It sounds like a soap opera, doesn't it? You know that when Laban went to bed that night, he must have said to his wife, "Wait until Jacob discovers what I've done. It is going to be unbelievable."

When Jacob realized he had been deceived, Laban tried to legitimize the whole affair by saying it was the custom that he couldn't give away his younger daughter until he had given away his older daughter.

But Laban had another deal for Jacob. "Finish [Leah's]

bridal week; then we will give you [Rachel] also, in return for another seven years of work" (v. 27). Such was Jacob's passionate love for Rachel that he said, "Fine, it's a deal." So Jacob married Rachel too.

Joseph's Family

With Jacob's marriages, the family album of Joseph began to fill up. The dining room was regularly in need of extra chairs. Jacob favored Rachel, but God closed her womb and opened the womb of Leah. God is sovereign in the details of life.

In rapid succession the Bible describes how the first twelve children of Jacob were born—eleven sons and a daughter. Altogether, Leah bore Jacob six sons and the only daughter, Dinah. Leah also gave her maidservant Zilpah to Jacob, and through her Jacob had two more sons.

When Rachel could not conceive, she gave *her* maidservant Bilhah to Jacob, and Bilhah bore two sons. Finally, in Genesis 30:22–24 we read, "God remembered Rachel . . . and opened her womb. She became pregnant and gave birth to a son. . . . She named him Joseph."

This was quite a family! One father, four mothers, two who were wives and two who were concubines, eleven sons, and one daughter. And at the end of this mixed-up, complicated family Joseph arrived, for the present the youngest of Jacob's sons. (Benjamin would not be born for several years, and in giving birth to him, Rachel would die [35:16–18]).

Between Joseph's birth and his appearance on the scene for good in Genesis 37:2 his name appears only three times, and in each of those he is given the barest mention (33:2, 7; 35:24). But he was part of the family during the events recorded in Genesis 31–36, which cover the first seventeen years of his life.

JOSEPH'S FORMATIVE YEARS

These were Joseph's formative years, a part of God's providential work to mold him for the future God had for him. God was already forming Joseph's character for an exceptional, sovereign purpose that neither he nor any of the others in his family would understand for many years.

So by way of summary, let's look at what happened to this lad and his family during the years between his birth and the real beginning of his story. What a record it is.

The Family's Flight from Laban

Sometime after Joseph was born, Jacob decided it was time to go back home and face his brother Esau in Canaan. We don't know how old Joseph was at this time—maybe six or seven years old. If so, he was old enough to take in his father's announcement across the dinner table, "We're moving back to Canaan."

Joseph probably didn't understand what it all meant, but he would have known that a big change was under way. One of his earliest recollections as a child must have been the hurried flight from the home of his grandfather Laban as Jacob took his family and flocks and left by night without Laban's knowledge (31:17–21).

I remember all the questions from the children when our family moved from Scotland to the United States. "When are we going? How are we going to get there? What will we do when we get there?"

When we arrived in the United States, the children didn't know where they were. When we went on vacation, they thought they were going home. They just couldn't process all the information involved in a big move like that. Their tiny lives were in an amazing whirl.

The experience of his family's flight to Canaan would have been much the same for Joseph. The family left under the cover of darkness so they wouldn't be detected. Jacob knew that if Laban found out they were leaving, he would try to stop them. And so in the moonlight little Joseph was put on a camel with his mother, and the large caravan started out toward Canaan.

I can hear Joseph asking Jacob, "Father, why are we running

away at night? Don't you like Grandfather? Doesn't Grandfather love us? Shouldn't we say good-bye to him?"

And then days later, when Laban caught up with the family (vv. 22–23), I wonder if Joseph was standing on the fringe listening as his grandfather looked at his father and said:

> *"What have you done? You've deceived me, and you've carried off my daughters like captives in war. Why did you run off secretly and deceive me? Why didn't you tell me, so I could send you away with joy and singing to the music of tambourines and harps? You didn't even let me kiss my grandchildren and my daughters good-by. You have done a foolish thing."* (vv. 26–28)

Now I don't know about your relationship with your grandfather, but my grandpa and I were as close as we could be. He never drove a car, as a result of wounds he had suffered in the First World War, and so we became experts in public transport in Glasgow. I've been on just about every bus to every terminus in the system.

I would ride the buses with my grandpa just to go places with him. At other times Grandpa and I would ride the whole subway system maybe three times, going nowhere, just me sitting beside him, listening to his stories. So I wouldn't want anybody tearing me away from my grandpa without the chance to kiss him good-bye.

But that's what happened to Joseph. He was going to have a lot of tearing away in his life—many times when he didn't get to say good-bye. He was going to have to learn how to weep and how to deal with pain. And even in these early life circumstances, God was forming Joseph in preparation for what was to come.

The final scene in Genesis 31 is one we need to etch onto our memories as far as the life of Joseph is concerned. Jacob and Laban made a covenant together then had a meal to seal the agreement, and Laban spent the night before going back home (vv. 43–54).

I want you to sense the emotion here. If you have ever moved a great distance from home, you know this "night before" experience well. The family is gathered, and there is a great reunion. But the joy is clouded by the prospect of the next morning and the separation.

So it was in Joseph's family. The text tells us, "Early the next morning Laban kissed his grandchildren and his daughters and blessed them. Then he left and returned home" (v. 55). Don't you think Laban squeezed those boys, maybe giving little Joseph an extra hug as the baby of the clan?

The Meeting with Esau

That part of the story comes to an end without any arguments or ugly scenes, but Jacob's distress was just beginning. Now he had to face the dreaded prospect of meeting his brother, Esau, who was coming to meet him with four hundred men. Fear gripped Jacob's heart at the very thought (32:7).

Again, Joseph would have been in on this to some degree. He may not have grasped the whole picture, but he knew something was wrong. He knew his father was afraid. Maybe he heard Jacob and Rachel talking in the tent, the way my mom and dad used to talk as they did the dishes. I would listen from the doorway, and I knew when my dad was troubled. And that is an apt word to describe Jacob's state in a very personal encounter with God.

You'll remember that Jacob divided his family and possessions and sent them on ahead. Separated from his family and his possessions, he encountered God in a surprising, personal, necessary way, and the result was permanent. He received a new name and a whole new identity.

In the morning, when Jacob returned to his family, he was limping as a result of his wrestling match with the Angel of the Lord. I don't know if he ever told Joseph what had happened that night, but the event had clearly stamped Jacob, for when the family got to Shechem, Jacob (now called Israel) built an altar to the Lord to set his family apart from the surrounding culture (33:18–20).

The Tragedy at Shechem

We are sketching in large strokes the background scenes of Joseph's life from birth to the age of seventeen, when his story begins in earnest. Joseph's father, Jacob (later called Israel), was reconciled to his brother, Esau, but when the family camped at Shechem, a dreadful tale unfolded—Dinah was raped by a young man also named Shechem, and Simeon and Levi devised a fearful reprisal against the men of the city (34:1–31).

Joseph may have been eleven or twelve at this time, and we can imagine what went through his mind as he heard all the hushed conversations and the extreme agitation of his older brothers. In it all God was working to form the character of this lad.

From Shechem the clan moved on under God's orders to Bethel, where Jacob had stopped on his flight from Esau (35:1; cf. 28:10–22). Jacob built an altar there to purify his household, and then bereavement touched his home.

The Death of Rachel

First, a woman named Deborah, the nurse to Jacob's mother, Rebekah, died and was mourned (35:8). Then Jacob suffered the loss of his beloved wife Rachel as she was giving birth to Benjamin (v. 18).

The birth of Benjamin was a key moment in Joseph's life. As the next youngest, Joseph would have had the closest emotional ties to Benjamin. Besides this, they were the only sons of Rachel. But the day of Benjamin's birth was one during which joy and sorrow mingled as life had ebbed from Joseph's mother in her final pangs of childbirth.

So once again the threads of pain and sorrow and bereavement were woven into Joseph's life. Then he had to deal with the death of his grandfather, Isaac (35:29). Another funeral, another reminder of the frailty of life, the reality of death, and the necessity of faith.

THE GRACE OF GOD

There is much more in these chapters that will reward your careful study. When we arrive at chapter 37, the camera lens is focused upon Joseph as the central person in the narrative. Now we are ready to look into the eyes of a young man of seventeen who has already been through more excitement and intrigue and trauma than most of us will experience in a lifetime.

In modern-day terms, Joseph came from a dysfunctional family. Indeed, we all came from a dysfunctional background because sin makes people dysfunctional. But when you take all the sins of a large number of selfish people and mix them together in a family, you have an entity badly out of alignment with wheels turning in different directions.

We can summarize this background briefly. We need to remember that in the rough-and-tumble of a less-than-perfect family life, God was preparing Joseph for the role He had planned for him. As a matter of fact, the only explanation for the life of Joseph and the role he played is found in the electing grace of God. There is no human reason whatsoever that Joseph should have emerged from the emotional and spiritual carnage of his family life to be the incredible man of God he was. The only way we can explain it is to say God purposed that it should be so. "God moves in a mysterious way, His wonders to perform. He plants His footsteps in the sea and rides upon the storm."

We mustn't allow our circumstances and disappointments to become the excuse for the choices we make in life. God is greater than all of that, and He can bring beauty out of ashes. Our trials come, Augustine said, "to prove us and to improve us." The mosaic of Joseph's background also provides us with a striking reminder of the impact a father's life has on his children.

Jacob was not a good model of integrity. He did poorly

when it came to decisiveness. He was slow when it came to action. He tended to avoid issues rather than face them. But God chose to use this imperfect father to raise the boy He had chosen to redeem His people from famine through his experiences in Egypt.

What of us parents? What is the legacy we are leaving? What stories will our children tell? When they stand and gaze at our tombstone, what then? Be encouraged that out of the chaos of Joseph's background came a man God used as a stirring example of His grace.

𝒜 NEW COAT, BIG DREAMS, AND A LONG TRIP

By the time Joseph reached the age of seventeen, he had seen more of the ugly side of family life than many people experience in a lifetime.

Given all the events that had unfolded in his life, Joseph was quite a remarkable seventeen year old. His background was prosperous, his family was large, and it was apparent that he was living with an increasing sense that somehow, in some way, God had something special planned for him.

Here in the early verses of Genesis 37, in the beginning of God's dealings with Joseph, we have the first inklings of God's providential care. We begin to see the unfolding of a classic Old Testament illustration of Romans 8:28, namely, that "in all things God works for the good of those who love him, who have been called according to his purpose."

Three aspects of Joseph's life set the tempo for all that followed. We discover that Joseph is the object of his father's special interest, his brothers' jealous hatred, and God's providential care.

THE OBJECT OF JACOB'S SPECIAL INTEREST

It was clear from the beginning that Joseph was the favorite of his father Jacob. "Now Israel [the new name given to Jacob] loved Joseph more than any of his other sons, because he had been born to him in his old age" (Genesis 37:3).

The Fact of Jacob's Favoritism

That's the fact of the case as it is given to us. Was it right? No. Playing favorites among one's children can be devastating to a family.

But this is the way it was for Jacob. Joseph was his baby boy, born in his old age to his great lifetime love, Rachel. It is easy to see how Jacob would have had a unique sense of affection for this young lad—and, in one sense, we should not be surprised at it.

After all, as children grow up and start going out on their own, the parents are left behind. Here was Jacob, wondering who he would spend time with, when he was given this gift of another boy. So everywhere the old man went, his young boy went also. They became constant companions. This elderly father especially loved his tender-aged child.

Jacob's other ten sons were much older than Joseph. They had established lives of their own by that time: They might have expected that Jacob would become attached to Joseph, and they might have understood that it was no judgment against them for their baby brother to become the object of his father's love.

John Calvin put it like this, "Sons of a more robust age, by dictate of nature, might well concede such a point." But clearly, Joseph's brothers didn't concede anything of the kind. And they did not share their father's love for their brother.

Jacob's favoritism might not have been so bad if it had

stopped there. But he gave Joseph an expensive gift, a "richly ornamented robe" (v. 3) that became a visible reminder to the brothers of Joseph's favored status. They hated him for it.

Why would a coat engender such hostility? Parents should be able to take one of their children shopping and buy something for that child without expecting the purchase to produce a venomous and treacherous response in the hearts of the other children.

Indeed, if a gift to another can cause that kind of response in people, they have a problem far deeper than the gift. And we discover that this was the case with Joseph's brothers.

It wasn't so much that the coat was very valuable, although I'm sure it was a splendid piece of workmanship. Nor was the problem that the coat was a display of Jacob's special affection for Joseph, for doubtless there were other ways the older brothers were picking that up.

The problem was that the coat put Joseph in a class apart. There was something about Joseph's wearing of the coat that spoke of leadership—a leadership that wouldn't naturally fall to the youngest son in the house. Reuben, Jacob's oldest son, should have inherited the leadership of the family. But Reuben had violated his father's confidence when he slept with Bilhah, one of his father's concubines (35:22). So as Jacob thought about the transition of leadership within his home, it was natural that he would turn to the son of his affection. And although Joseph was only a teenager, he was already establishing himself as a person of character and trustworthiness. In giving Joseph this lovely coat, his father set him apart.

Every time Joseph put that coat on, his brothers must have said, "We hate that coat and we hate him!" This was the result of Jacob's favoritism.

The Folly of Jacob's Favoritism

Even though God's providence was continually overruling in Joseph's life, we need to recognize that Jacob's actions were unwise. It is poor judgment for a father to display favoritism among his children, especially in such an overt and striking fashion as was represented by Joseph's coat.

Jacob's favoritism is particularly worth noting because of his own background. His relationship with his brother, Esau, had been destroyed for years by the favoritism of Isaac and Rebekah.

Genesis 25:28 is a sad verse. "Isaac, who had a taste for wild game, loved Esau, but Rebekah loved Jacob." It was Rebekah's scheming to advance her favorite son that plunged the family into chaos.

You would think those painful memories would have prevented Jacob from making the same mistake with his sons. Not so. History repeats itself. Jacob probably thought, *I know Esau wanted to kill me, but I won't let anything happen to Joseph.*

But we are not in control of events. So let me stop here and send a memo to parents: Beware the folly of favoritism and the fury that so often accompanies it. All of our children are unique gifts from God. We need to cherish each child with obvious love and affection, recognizing each child's unique personality, individual capabilities, and special needs.

Joseph may have been the light of Jacob's life, but by singling out Joseph for special favors, Jacob did nothing but cast dark, destructive shadows over his beloved son's life. Favoritism within a family is a foolishness that leads to fury.

THE OBJECT OF HIS BROTHERS' HATRED

Not only did Joseph enjoy his father's special blessing, he had to endure his brothers' scheming bitterness. He was the object of his brothers' jealous hatred. And hatred it was!

There is a progression in the text. We are told in Genesis 37:4, "When [Joseph's] brothers saw that their father loved him more than any of them, they hated him and could not speak a kind word to him."

Then when Joseph told the brothers his dream, "they hated

him all the more" (vv. 5, 8). Finally, we read, "His brothers were jealous of him" (v. 11).

It wasn't that Joseph's older brothers simply didn't like him. It wasn't that they were irritated because their father made them take Joseph along with them. Most of us can remember that scenario. "Let your brother play with you. It won't hurt you to do that." No, this was much more than irritation at a little brother. The ten older boys had an intense hatred for Joseph that would express itself in immense cruelty toward him. The narrative makes clear the three factors that contributed to this hatred.

They Hated Him for His Bad Report

The brothers' hatred of Joseph was initially provoked by the "bad report about them" he brought to Jacob (v. 2). There's little doubt that the closeness Joseph enjoyed with his father would encourage this kind of talebearing.

There is no hint here that Joseph was motivated by unkindness. The fact of his report is simply stated. If there was a legitimate reason for it, that's one thing. If there wasn't, and Joseph was making it all up, that was wrong. But what we have read of his brothers in the previous chapters of Genesis leads us to believe that there was plenty of reason for the report.

Whatever had happened, Joseph noted the unacceptable behavior of his older brothers and reported it to their father, much like any teenager might do.

As a boy in Scotland, I admired my friend Graham's older brother, who served in the Royal Navy. I was enamored with his uniform and his muscles and his stories.

However, some of his tales were unhelpful, and I recall Graham going to his dad and giving a bad report about his brother. "Do you know what he was saying? Do you know what he did in Singapore?" The older brother quickly determined it would be better for him to be back in the navy than to hang around with his kid brother, who got him in trouble with his father.

That's probably the way it went for Joseph and his brothers. He reported their bad behavior, and they didn't like it.

They Hated Him for His Coat

We have already mentioned this reason for the brothers' hatred. The text says they could not speak kindly to Joseph. Their eyes never met his at the dinner table. They couldn't engage Joseph in conversation without hatred and venom spilling out.

The root of this hatred was clear. Joseph's brothers were flat-out jealous of him. There are people who have not spoken or written to their brothers and sisters in years because of the monster called jealousy.

Jealousy *is* a monster, a giant that will eat us alive. The happiness and success of others is poison to the bloodstream of the jealous.

That's why it's almost easier to get demoted in your work than to get promoted, for when you get promoted it reveals the character of the people around you. It's hard for people to come to you and say, "I am so pleased that you got this wonderful promotion ahead of me, and I'm glad that you are now above me in the pecking order."

Let's be honest. It's *very* hard to do that. So before we get on our spiritual high horse and condemn Joseph's brothers, let's remember that the hat with "Jealousy" written across the front often fits perfectly on our heads too.

Did you know that pastors can get jealous of one another? F. B. Meyer, a great British preacher earlier in this century, told how his fellow great preacher G. Campbell Morgan came to preach in the same location as Meyer. Gradually, people began drifting from Meyer's congregation into Morgan's.

Meyer later wrote of how envy and jealousy began to grip his soul, and how the only liberation he could find was to pray for Campbell Morgan and ask God to bless his ministry. Meyer prayed that God would bless Morgan's ministry so much there wouldn't be enough seats to hold all the people who wanted to hear him—and that they would come and listen to F. B. Meyer.

A Scottish commentator of two hundred years ago said, "The odious passion of jealousy torments and destroys oneself, while it seeks the ruin of its object." Jealousy destroys the jealous person, not the object of envy. It's like self-pity. It eats you up, but it doesn't do anything to the other person.

Ancient Greek history tells the story of a statue erected in a prominent position in a certain city to honor a famous athlete.

A rival athlete, who was jealous of the success of his colleague, decided that he would destroy that statue. So he came at night with hammer and chisel, chipping away at the foundation of the statue, hoping to weaken it and bring it down.

He finally weakened the statue enough that it fell—but on him, crushing him to death. If we're going to avoid the folly of favoritism, we need also to make sure we don't end up in the jail of jealousy.

If Joseph's brothers had understood that God sovereignly works in peoples' lives and that He had sovereignly determined to make Joseph the object of His favor, they might have had no occasion to be envious. Or at least they might have been able to understand God's perspective of what was happening, even if it still bothered them.

God sets people up and brings people down. So the people who are raised up mustn't get fat heads, and the people who aren't raised up mustn't get discouraged. If only Joseph's brothers had fastened on this truth, they would have saved themselves and their whole family much heartache.

Someone expressed this truth in a little couplet: "It takes more grace than I can tell, to play the second fiddle well." That's the hardest position to play.

John the Baptist played it well. He occupies a central position in the opening chapters of the Gospel of John. He was the forerunner to Christ, preaching repentance and baptizing great numbers of people and having quite a successful ministry.

But John understood his role. So when his disciples came and told him he was losing his crowd to this man Jesus, John replied, "A man can receive only what is given him from heaven" (John 3:27). John knew God had made him a voice, not the Word. He knew God had made him a forerunner, not the Messiah. And he knew God had made him a herald, not the King.

We can translate this into whatever arena of life in which we operate. The answer to avoiding jealousy is in 1 Corinthians 4:7. "Who makes you different from anyone else? What do you have that you did not receive? [Answer: nothing]. And if you did receive it, why do you boast as though you did not?"

They Hated Him for His Dreams

Besides his bad report and his beautiful coat, Joseph was hated by his brothers because of his dreams. Now, obviously, these were no ordinary dreams.

Everybody dreams. Some people remember their dreams and some don't, and at the breakfast table most dreams are good for a laugh. We decide we are going to have to stop eating so much before we go to bed because of the crazy stuff we dream about.

Joseph's brothers could have done that. They could have laughed when he said to them, "Listen to this dream I had: We were binding sheaves of grain out in the field when suddenly my sheaf rose and stood upright, while your sheaves gathered around mine and bowed down to it" (Genesis 37:6–7).

The brothers could have listened to that and said, "Oh man, he's crazy. What a dumb idea. Look at Joseph with his silly dreams and his silly coat."

The reason the ten brothers didn't do that was because it was obvious that God was somehow involved in those dreams. They were portents of what God would do. God was speaking by means of dreams so that when the events unfolded as dreamed, it would be apparent to everybody that they had not happened fortuitously, but as the unfolding of God's plan. So it was that Joseph told his brothers his extraordinary dream.

But that wasn't the end of it. Joseph said, "I had another dream, and this time the sun and moon and eleven stars were bowing down to me" (v. 9).

Should Joseph have shared his dreams? Probably not. It may have been an error of judgment to tell his brothers these things. Later, Joseph told his father the second dream and was rebuked for it (v. 10). But within these dreams was the strong hint that Joseph was the object of God's special favor and the servant of His special purpose.

Because of the dreams, Joseph's brothers intensified their hatred of him. Imagine being seventeen and knowing that no one really likes you. Do you remember when you were seventeen? Do you remember how important approval was to you? It was everything. The last thing in the world you wanted to be was isolated, to walk the corridors at school with no one to talk to and no one to hang out with, no point of identification beyond yourself.

That's the worst possible predicament for a teenager, but it was Joseph's predicament. We would not have been surprised if Joseph had emerged from this experience withdrawn and inward-looking, hiding in his room listening to music, to put it in modern terms.

But look at him. Joseph was resilient, focused, clear. His brothers' hatred and his father's rebuke did not shrivel his character.

JOSEPH WAS THE OBJECT
OF GOD'S PROVIDENTIAL CARE

The resilience of his personality was surely grounded in a growing awareness that in and through it all he was the object of God's providential care.

To our earlier definition of providence we add that which is provided by the Heidelberg Catechism. "Providence is the almighty and ever-present power of God by which he upholds, as with his hand, heaven and earth and all creatures, and so rules them that leaf and blade, rain and drought, fruitful and lean years, food and drink, health and sickness, prosperity and poverty—all things, in fact, come to us not by chance but from his fatherly hand." God was providentially involved in the events of Joseph's life, as was made obvious in his trip to visit his brothers.

The Danger of His Trip

One day Israel (Jacob) sent Joseph to check on his brothers, who were grazing the family's flocks some distance away (Genesis 37:12). "Israel said to Joseph, 'As you know, your brothers are grazing the flocks near Shechem. Come, I am going to send you to them.' 'Very well,' he replied" (v. 13).

Joseph might have answered, "Please don't send me. Couldn't you send a servant? Don't you realize my brothers hate me? They never talk to me. It will be terrible when they see me. Besides, Shechem is miles away." But Joseph obeyed his father, knowing it was going to be a rough trip.

I don't know how tuned-in Jacob was when he sent Joseph on this journey. Did Jacob realize he was putting his boy in jeopardy? Did he realize there was danger in the journey in more ways than one? Are we to assume that by this time he paid little attention to what was going on around him and was only superficially aware of the hatred his older boys had for his younger son?

We don't know. It's easier to understand Jacob's decision on the basis that he really didn't think the older boys would do anything to harm Joseph.

That's understandable. Lots of parents say, "Oh, sure, the boys fight once in a while. But they would never hurt each other." So Jacob sent Joseph off with a pat on the back. "You'll be fine. Go on now. Find your brothers."

If Jacob had realized that when Joseph left for Shechem, the back of his head was the last Jacob would see of his beloved boy for twenty years, I'm not sure he would have sent him. But God was in control of the circumstances, and it was actually better for Joseph to be isolated from his home but in the center of God's plan, than to be at home but isolated from God's purposes.

We make a mistake when we try to determine God's guidance on the basis of what is the most comfortable, acceptable, and rational to us. God's providential dealings will overrule even in the fracturings and separations and jealousies of life.

The Plot of His Brothers

Picture the scene as Joseph approached his brothers in the fields near Dothan (vv. 14–18). He had gone to Shechem but was told by a stranger he met that the brothers had talked about moving on to Dothan. Shechem was fifty miles from Hebron. Dothan was another fifteen miles away.

As Joseph finally approached his brothers over all those miles of rugged terrain, they got him in their sights. "'Here comes that dreamer!' they said to each other. 'Come now, let's kill him'" (vv. 19–20).

Don't miss the irony of this. As the ten older brothers sat and watched Joseph appear on the horizon, they recognized his coat and plotted to kill the very person without whom, someday, they would starve to death. "He who was ordained to be the minister of their salvation is *about to be* thrown into a well" (Calvin).

We can see the irony because we know that God was purposing to take Joseph into Egypt for the preservation of his family in the day of famine. But for now the brothers wanted to kill the only person who could save them.

SOME CLOSING OBSERVATIONS

The unfolding drama of Joseph's life is already providing us with principles to ponder. Let us recognize again that God was as firmly in control of the plots and the pits of Joseph's life as He was in control of Joseph's dreams and their fulfillment.

"Judge not the Lord by feeble sense, nor try His works in vain. God is His own interpreter, and He will make things plain," the hymnist has said.

When you or your loved one is rolled into the hospital room for a CAT scan and the doctor says the news is bad, the temptation is to ask, "Where is God in all of this?" The answer is that He is as sovereignly in control of "all of this" as He is in control of the blessings in our lives.

We need to learn from Joseph not to be grieved when God determines to prosper us and others become jealous. This is a hard lesson for many people to learn. I often hear people trying to discount and explain away God's blessing so that others won't be upset with them.

But there's no need for it! If you realize that God enabled you to put the business deal together and smiled on it, if you know that the very breath you breathe is a gift from God's hand, and if you can only explain the bottom line in terms of God's sovereign choice to bless you, you don't need to bury yourself because the next guy is jealous of your success.

Listen to Calvin again: "Let us not be grieved, if at any time the shining of the grace of God upon us should cause us to be envied." If Joseph's brothers had a grievance, it was with Jacob. Joseph never asked for the coat. Nor did he conjure up the dreams.

Third, note that God's providential care expresses itself in wonderful and unusual ways. Joseph was about to be tossed into a cistern, but God would shine the light of victory and power and provision into that dark hole. So we mustn't look upon the dark and disappointing times of our lives as those that thwart the unfolding of God's purpose. We must learn to trust Him, even in the dark.

P. S. Do we see the wonderful and dramatic way in which these events, and Joseph himself, foreshadow Another who was to come?

- As it was on account of envy that Joseph was handed into slavery, so Matthew tells us that Pilate recognized in the actions of the Jewish leaders that "it was out of envy that they had handed Jesus over to him" (Matthew 27:18).

- As Joseph traveled across the hill country in search of those who would reject him, so Jesus "came to that which was his own, but his own did not receive him" (John 1:11).

- As Joseph was despised and rejected by those he would one day rescue, so Jesus' experience of rejection was to become the gateway to life for all who believe.

Chapter Three

SOLD, SAD, AND SAFE

There is probably no greater single illustration of God's providence at work in a life than what we're discovering in this unfolding drama. Joseph has just walked into the sights of ten cruel, hateful elder brothers.

But he was not at the mercy of fate or chance. He was not being driven along by a blind, impersonal force. He was under the watchful eye of his sovereign God.

Verse 18 of Genesis 37 says that Joseph's brothers saw him coming from a distance. How did they know it was he? Was it the peculiar way he walked, the way he swung his head from side to side, or some other trait? We don't know, but it's most likely they recognized Joseph because of his special coat.

"'Here comes that dreamer!' they said to each other. 'Come now, let's kill him and throw him into one of these cisterns and say that a ferocious animal devoured him. Then we'll see what comes of his dreams'" (vv. 19–20).

We can imagine them remarking, "We'll see if Joseph does any more dreaming after we get through with him!"

Joseph's brothers had sown the seeds of hatred in their hearts, and those seeds had found fertile soil. The brothers had watered the seeds with jealousy and cultivated them with selfishness. Now the seeds began to bear their bitter fruit. Their hatred toward Joseph was disproportionate to any of his offenses against them.

Their determination to kill him is a reminder that hatred doesn't need a reason. All it needs is a corner of a selfish heart in which to germinate.

JOSEPH WAS SPARED BY REUBEN

When the eldest brother, Reuben, heard that the plan was to kill Joseph and hide his body in a deep well, he intervened with another plan. He proposed an amendment to the motion. "Let's not take his life. . . . Throw him into this cistern here in the desert, but don't lay a hand on him" (vv. 21–22). His plan was to create a situation that would make it possible for him to come back later and rescue Joseph from the cistern and take him home to Jacob (v. 22). So he was motivated by the best of reasons.

The other brothers went along with Reuben's suggestion, not knowing that he was planning to rescue Joseph later. They stripped their little brother of his coat and threw him into the dry cistern (vv. 23–24).

This may seem mildly compassionate on their part, but there's nothing truly nice about the brothers' response. If you think about it, killing Joseph and then tossing his body into the cistern would have been more humane than throwing him into the cistern alive and leaving him there in the desert to die a slow and agonizing death of dehydration and starvation.

We shouldn't imagine for a moment that the brothers agreed to Reuben's suggestion because they thought it was a kinder and gentler way to treat Joseph. Perhaps they had a small twinge of conscience as they thought about the ramifications of their actions, but that was about the extent of it. As we're about to see, their subsequent actions demonstrated the callousness of their hearts.

Reuben's Purpose

It's interesting that Reuben was the one who purposed to

save Joseph. Do you remember the last time the camera of God's Word zoomed in on Reuben's face? It is recorded in Genesis 35:22 that Reuben dishonored God, his father, his father's concubine Bilhah, and himself by sleeping with her.

Reuben's sin was heinous, so instinctively we assume that he was a bad apple. Anyone who sinned in that manner against his father and his family couldn't be particularly nice.

But was Reuben incapable of genuine compassion and sympathy? In seeking to save Joseph, was he motivated by something other than genuine concern? Some Bible commentators suggest that Reuben acted in this way because he saw a chance to balance out his iniquity and regain Jacob's favor. If Reuben took Joseph back to Jacob and explained what "the naughty nine" had planned to do to the dreamer, and that he had intervened to save him, then maybe Jacob would think well of Reuben again.

But as George Lawson says, "Let not the worst of men be found worse than they really are." The fact that he was enticed in the area of lust doesn't mean that he was incapable of compassion in his heart for his youngest brother. All of us have our own particular areas of sin.

When we are all alone with nobody watching, do we gravitate toward despair and discouragement? Lust and impurity? Or perhaps we are prone to jealousy or bitterness. We need to be honest in identifying where we are vulnerable.

The apostle James says we succumb to temptation when we are enticed and led away by our "own evil desire" (James 1:14). All of us face temptation, but not all of us are tempted by the same things.

It is not necessary to read Reuben's actions in Genesis 37 solely in light of his failure in chapter 35. He may indeed have been broken by the earlier events and was crying out for an opportunity to do something that would express his repentance to his father. Combined with Reuben's genuine concern for Joseph, it is understandable why he was so distraught when he came back later and found Joseph gone (37:29–30). Yet in all of this spiritual darkness, jealousy, and cruelty, God's hand of providence remained on Joseph's life.

JOSEPH WAS SOLD BY JUDAH

Imagine Joseph's terror and confusion as his brothers cold-heartedly pulled him out of the cistern and sold him to the Midianite merchants for twenty shekels of silver. We almost have to squeeze our eyes a bit and squint to believe what we find in these verses. Remember when you looked at a picture in art class, and you were supposed to see certain images or other things? But you weren't seeing anything until the art teacher told you, "Squeeze your eyes and squint at the picture." So you did that, and somehow from that perspective you could see the outline of certain things you didn't see before.

The Coldhearted Brothers

That's how I find myself approaching this part of the story.

It is incredible that brothers in the same earthly family could treat one of their own the way these brothers treated Joseph. It is even more incredible that they could sit down and eat a meal after doing the dirty deed. But that's exactly what they did (v. 25).

This is an ugly, cruel picture. They stripped Joseph of his coat—and we can be sure it wasn't with a polite, "May I take your coat for you, Joseph?" Rather, they grabbed him, tore the coat off, and threw him into the pit—fully intending to let their teenage brother die in that hole.

That was bad enough. But, then, in an expression of the calluses encrusting their hearts, "they sat down to eat their meal" (v. 25).

What does it take to spoil your appetite? Some people can eat like horses anytime. But most people have faced occasions when their emotions were so overwrought they said, "I just can't eat. Maybe when I get over this, but not now."

You stand outside your loved one's room at the hospital, or

you walk up and down the hall while the surgery is in progress, and as you wait someone offers you something to eat, and you say, "Thanks a lot, but I can't eat just now."

Those meals held after a funeral are so helpful for the people who have come from a distance, and they are an opportunity for fellowship. But I've observed something. The widow or widower doesn't usually eat much.

But when we see men who can tear the clothes off the back of their seventeen-year-old brother, throw him down a hole in the ground, and leave him there to die, and then turn around and say, "Hey, has anyone got ketchup for these fries?" it is clear that we are plumbing the depths of depravity.

Judah's Suggestion

Judah's intervention resulted in Joseph's sentence being commuted from death to perpetual slavery. When the brothers looked up and saw some foreign traders coming their way, Judah saw an opportunity.

So he asked the others, "What will we gain if we kill our brother and cover up his blood?" (v. 26). The others were at least sensible enough to realize Judah was right. They weren't going to gain a lot by killing Joseph. So the question registered.

Judah followed up with a suggestion. "Come, let's sell him to the Ishmaelites and not lay our hands on him; after all, he is our brother, our own flesh and blood" (v. 27). Judah was having a little twinge of conscience himself.

So they pulled Joseph out of the cistern and sold him to the traders on the caravan for twenty shekels of silver (v. 28). The price didn't amount to much, just a couple of shekels each for the brothers' dirty work. It is hard to imagine that they enjoyed whatever it was they bought with their ill-gotten gain.

The Brothers' Lie

So that was it. The deed was done. Joseph was gone by the time Reuben returned, and now the brothers had to go home and face their father. So they came up with the deceitful idea of dipping Joseph's coat in animal blood, presenting it to Jacob, and letting him draw the obvious conclusion (vv. 31–33). It was a deception the brothers would maintain for some twenty years.

There is an important lesson here. It is virtually impossible to commit just one sin. One sin needs another to guard it from detection. How many more lies do you think the brothers had to tell over the next two decades to keep up the sham? Jacob must have grilled them about the incident. Surely other family members and friends asked them to recount the story.

You can mark it down that when you sin, you'll sin again, especially in the area of lying. When a person is prepared to kill, don't be surprised if he will tell thousands of lies to protest his innocence and shield himself from the shame of his actions. It is to be expected.

Therefore, it was no surprise that these brothers, who were capable of the grossest kind of cruelty toward Joseph, were also guilty of the worst kind of hypocrisy and duplicity toward their father. They watched him plunge into a grief so deep it almost put him in his grave (v. 35), and yet they kept on lying.

We dare not miss the challenge to become men and women marked by integrity and honesty. God's Word makes clear that if we start trading in lies, our sin will destroy our lives. Become a liar and you will weave a web for yourself that will strangle you in the end and trip up countless others in the process.

People who lie in their business dealings are in the worst of positions. Their integrity is shot and their conscience is defiled and ruined. They drive themselves crazy trying to figure out what other people are thinking, saying, and doing—because they assume everyone else is lying too.

Lies are like a strand of sewing thread wrapped around your fingers. One strand is so easy to break you don't think anything of it. You say to yourself, "That wasn't so bad. I got away with it. I told a lie and nobody found out."

So you lie again, only this time there are two strands of thread around your fingers. Then you add a third and a fourth—and before long, your fingers are so tied up you can't use your hand anymore.

We must beware of developing such a pattern in our lives. It will keep us from usefulness in God's kingdom, and it may even keep us from the kingdom itself. Joseph's brothers remind us that there is no cistern deep enough and no amount of time long enough to hide our sin from the eyes of an all-seeing God.

There is only one way to deal with the sin that weaves its web of destruction around our soul: repent of it, be done with it, and ask God's help to liberate ourselves from it.

JOSEPH WAS SAD IN HIS HEART

When Joseph was sold into slavery, he felt horror at what was happening to him.

This is a case in which we can't let our familiarity with the story dull our human sensitivities. This is a seventeen-year-old boy who was brutalized by his brothers, ripped from his family by force, and then sold to foreign slave traders.

When we were seventeen most of us were trying to figure out who we were and what we were going to become. But it was also an exciting time. We had our driver's license and the world was at our feet.

But ask Joseph, "What stands out about your seventeenth year?"

"That's easy," he would answer. "That was the year my father sent me to Shechem for what was supposed to be a few days to check on my brothers. But I didn't see my family again for twenty years.

"In my wildest dreams—and I had some pretty wild dreams—I couldn't have imagined I would end up like that. I couldn't believe my brothers hated me that much. They threw me into a deep pit.

"I cried in that pit. I cried for mercy; I pled for my life.

They pulled me out of the cistern, but sold me to strangers who put me on the back of a mangy camel and took me off to Egypt. I cried on the back of that camel.

"And every time I turned and looked down that dusty path, I wondered if my dad would come with his men to rescue me and take me home. All I wanted to do was go home. But nobody came, and I was gone."

That's what Joseph might say. Was he really that distressed? Yes, according to Genesis 42:21. As that verse records, his brothers were talking to one another in a different setting, recalling what it was like when they threw him into the pit. "Surely we are being punished because of our brother. We saw how distressed he was when he pleaded with us for his life, but we would not listen; that's why this distress has come upon us."

Joseph was sold and sad. But those are not the final words.

JOSEPH WAS SAFE IN GOD'S HAND

Joseph probably didn't feel very safe, tied up as a piece of property to be bought and sold and placed on the back of a camel for the journey to Egypt.

But Joseph *was* safe, because even though his earthly father stayed behind in Canaan, his heavenly Father came with him into Egypt. Sometimes the will of God is found on the back of a smelly camel going down to a far country.

I wonder what Joseph thought about on that trip. What sustained him during those days of fear and uncertainty? This is conjecture on my part, but I have an idea. Isn't it at least possible that one of the means God used to sustain Joseph in this time of deep trial was the memory of his grandfather's stories? Part of the privilege of being a grandparent lies in having access to the expanding minds of our children's children.

Any child who loves his grandpa, loves his grandpa's stories. A grandfather's knee may prove to be as influential a location as any classroom. "Grandpa, tell me about the old days when you were small." And the stories start coming.

Remember that Joseph's grandfather was Isaac. As that old man sorted through his memories, he would have recounted the story told in Genesis 22 of how his father, Abraham, had been commanded by God to offer him as a sacrifice on Mount Moriah.

Isaac must have told Joseph about his feelings as Abraham raised the knife, the miraculous provision of the ram caught in the thicket, and how it was that he, who was to be the sacrifice, walked free on account of God's provision.

Is it not reasonable to assume Isaac must have said to Joseph, "My son, if you will trust in the God of your great-grandfather Abraham, your grandfather Isaac, and your father, Jacob, you will discover that no matter what happens to you, no matter where you go, no matter how difficult life becomes, God Himself will provide for you."

Now whether or not it happened like that, there has to be an explanation for the way this boy went through his troubles and turned out as he did. Somehow, despite his extreme distress, Joseph must have been aware that God was still in control of his life. He was learning to say with the psalmist, "I am still confident of this: I will see the goodness of the Lord in the land of the living" (Psalm 27:13).

Joseph understood that even in the exercise of his brothers' hatred, God was working. Perhaps on his ride to Egypt Joseph recognized that God had already provided for him through the intervention of Reuben that saved his life and through Judah's suggestion that he be brought up alive out of the pit.

Perhaps Joseph realized it was only by the hand of God that his brothers had complied with those proposals. Nor was it by chance that a caravan of Ishmaelite merchants had arrived at just the right time for Judah to see them and suggest an alternative to the cruel plot the brothers had had in mind initially. Those traders had been there by divine appointment, and God had determined they would make the decision to buy the lad.

If we had asked Joseph's brothers, "Why did you sell him

into slavery?" they would have said, "To be rid of him and his lousy dreams."

If we had asked the Ishmaelite traders, "Why did you buy Joseph?" they would have said, "To turn a profit."

And yet as they served themselves and their own ends, the brothers and the traders did a great service to Joseph. Their selfish interests became, in God's providence, instrumental in saving Joseph's life and, ultimately, the lives of the brothers themselves.

So we are beginning to see that even when, as Calvin puts it, the world appears to be aimlessly walking about, the Lord is everywhere at work.

The center of God's will may take us into the eye of a storm. For Joseph the storm was the back of a smelly camel going down to Egypt. We should not seek to confirm God's will by the absence of adversity. Consider the staggering words written about Jesus in Isaiah 53:10: "Yet it was the Lord's will to crush him and cause him to suffer."

We take heart by recalling, "If God is for us, who can be against us?" (Romans 8:31). Ten bad-apple brothers and a whole caravan full of hard-eyed desert traders were no match for the teenage boy who appeared to be the helpless victim in the story; God was with him.

God will accomplish His purposes even though for the time being it might appear that everything has gone awry. There is no denying Joseph's distress at being sold and at anticipating the years of slavery and suffering that lay ahead of him. Those events are a reminder to us that, as the great pastor and author A. W. Tozer once said, "It is doubtful that God ever used anybody greatly without first hurting him deeply."

It takes the test of trials to make us useful to God. Some of us are not as useful as we might be, for in shunning the trials we have missed the blessings. We do not have the tender hearts that come from nights of tears. We don't seek the tears, but they will indeed come from the Father's hand. And they will come so that we might be prepared to accomplish His will in our lives and in the lives of others.

Look now at the scene as Jacob is pierced through as with a sword. Grief was not new to him, but this was a bitter blow. Joseph, that ray of sunshine in the depressing shadows created by his brothers, *gone!* And Jacob was the one who had sent him on that errand. As we leave the patriarch in tears, we remember that with God, joy comes in the morning. Under the shadow of God's hand His saints may dwell secure. Read on!

𝒜 DECISION TO MAKE

What a radical change has taken place in Joseph's life. He who was the object of the loving attention of a doting dad is now the object of curiosity to people in the market for a slave. The dreamer hits the dirt. Now that's dramatic. Joseph is about to discover that although he is a long way from everyone and everything that represents security, he is still hemmed in "behind and before" by God, and the hand of God still guides him and holds him fast (see Psalm 139:5, 10).

Some of our circumstances any of us has changed over a period of time, but it is unlikely that any of us has been taken so low so fast.

"Potiphar, an Egyptian who was one of Pharaoh's officials, the captain of the guard, bought [Joseph] from the Ishmaelites" (Genesis 39:1). This suggests a slave auction, an event that could not have been anything but ugly, distasteful, humiliating, and cruel for Joseph. Paraded on the slave block in full view of a leering crowd, perhaps stripped bare, he was offered for sale. There he stood, a teenager subjected to the proddings of his potential master.

Exposure to this kind of humiliation would have ripped into the core of Joseph's being. Try to get a sense of the pain and confusion he felt as he sought to understand what was happening to him. He was a captive in a foreign country, unable to understand the words spoken to him. He could only try to read their eyes and so figure out what they were thinking and planning.

Joseph didn't have to wait long to learn his fate. When the ordeal of the slave auction was over, he was taken—probably in chains and under guard—into the palatial home of Potiphar, a prominent Egyptian official.

To put this man's position in a modern context, we could say that Potiphar was the chief of Pharaoh's secret police. He was in charge of dealing with political insurrectionists. People who plotted against the Pharaoh were taken into custody by Potiphar and his men, never to be heard from again.

Potiphar's job was to remove threats to his boss. He was a powerful man and probably had the potential for cruelty. So it is an understatement to say that the circumstances into which Joseph was thrust were less than ideal.

Years later, reflecting upon Joseph's life, his father, Jacob, said, "With bitterness archers attacked him; they shot at him with hostility" (Genesis 49:23). This was a graphic picture of Joseph's vulnerability as hostile forces took potshots at him. He was exposed, alone, fearful, and wondering—and, yet, in the center of God's will.

Here we discover an essential and simple truth, which is this: There is no ideal place to serve God except the place in which He has set you down. There is no ideal job for you to hold, no ideal neighborhood in which to live, and no ideal church you can join.

There are good jobs, good neighborhoods, and good churches, but no ideal ones. People who search for ideal circumstances forget that all that is ideal and perfect is saved for heaven. They launch forth on a journey destined to end in disappointment. One of my goals in this book is to spare you from making such a journey.

Joseph's life at this point was far from ideal. He may have

been tempted to run away, give up, or become angry. But here we discover him making the most of his situation.

Responding to similar circumstances in his life, the psalmist said, "In the Lord I take refuge. How then can you say to me: 'Flee like a bird to your mountain'?" (Psalm 11:1).

Sometimes circumstances make us want to run. We say to ourselves, *If I could only get away for a while—maybe a weekend at the cabin or a few days at the beach.*

Refreshments and a vacation may be of temporary help, but we can't flee from ourselves. I don't know about you, but my biggest problem is not my circumstances, my colleagues, or my boss. My biggest problem is me.

We may think, *I never bargained for this. I never imagined being trapped in this mess.* No, we probably didn't. But God has chosen to set us down in this environment. Even in circumstances like those that surrounded Joseph, we can trace God's hand.

JOSEPH WAS PROTECTED

It was immediately apparent that Joseph was under the protecting hand of God.

We can see this hand in the way Joseph went from a death plot to the pit, where he surely would have died, and from the pit to the back of a camel. In all of this, he was still alive.

Joseph wasn't protected *from* the circumstances but *in* the circumstances. We often ask God to remove the problem from us or remove us from the problem. But most of the time what God does with His children is change their attitude toward the circumstances in which they find themselves.

God could have done things differently in Joseph's life. But God purposed that "through many dangers, toils, and snares" He would fashion His servant for noble service and erase the blemishes in his character, even as He is doing with us.

Protected by God's Presence

As we saw in the previous chapter, Joseph's heavenly Father

accompanied him to Egypt. God's presence was the source of the young man's protection.

Joseph would have agreed with the psalmist when he wrote, "The Lord is a refuge for the oppressed, a stronghold in times of trouble. Those who know your name will trust in you, for you, Lord, have never forsaken those who seek you" (Psalm 9:9–10). And, "God is our refuge and strength, an ever-present help in trouble" (Psalm 46:1).

When we find ourselves disappointed and broken and unable to alter our circumstances, we do well to go to the Bible, the soul's medicine chest. One of the best potions in the chest is the book of Psalms. As we read the psalmist's words, we realize again that his experience of God's presence is that for which we long.

Do you recall the experience of Moses leading the nation of Israel from Egypt? He was anxious and said to God, "You have not let me know whom you will send with me" (Exodus 33:12).

God said, "My Presence will go with you" (v. 14). Moses replied, "If your Presence does not go with us, do not send us up from here. How will anyone know that you are pleased with me and with your people unless you go with us?" (vv. 15–16).

It is the accompanying presence of God in the life of His servant that makes the servant distinctive. Somehow it is apparent to people that there is a different dimension in the life of God's servant; that dimension is the fact of His protecting presence. "The Lord was with Joseph" (Genesis 39:2).

Protected from Damaging Emotions

God also protected Joseph from human emotions that could easily have unraveled him.

It is not overtly stated in the text, but I think we can say with confidence that God protected Joseph from the silent killers of resentment, self-pity, and bitterness. Based on what had happened to him by this point, Joseph was a prime candidate for any or all of those powerful and destructive emotions.

Surely in those first nights of his slavery in Potiphar's

house, Joseph must have tossed and turned on his bed, his mind filled with confusion. He was a dreamer, remember.

Perhaps on some nights Joseph woke up in a sweat remembering in his mind's eye the hatred in the eyes of his brothers when they grabbed him and he pled not to be left in the cistern. When he awoke, the rattling of his chains reminded him that it was because of his brothers that he was a captive in a foreign land. In moments like that, deep resentment can begin to brew.

On other nights Joseph may have dreamed that he was back home with his father and his family and everything was fine again. He was laughing and talking with his loved ones—and then he awoke and returned to the reality of his circumstances. In the cruelty of missing his father and his wee brother, Benjamin, Joseph could have buried himself in self-pity and resentment.

Some of us know what it's like to feel trapped by our circumstances, victimized by the cruelty or neglect or insensitivity of others. We feel flashes of resentment urging us to take our revenge. Or we feel sorry for ourselves, or allow ourselves to become embittered.

How do we avoid these devastating emotions? By seeking God's protection from them. Joseph didn't allow himself to become imprisoned behind the walls of resentment, revenge, self-pity, or bitterness. We must do the same. In the circumstances each of us face, no matter how difficult our days, we must ask God for the strength to resist bitterness and nourish a gentle heart.

Paul says in Ephesians 4, "Do not let any unwholesome talk come out of your mouths, but only what is helpful for building others up according to their needs, that it may benefit those who listen. And do not grieve the Holy Spirit of God, with whom you were sealed for the day of redemption" (vv. 29–30).

How can we do that? He continues, "Get rid of all bitterness, rage and anger, brawling and slander, along with every form of malice" (v. 31).

You say, "But I can't." No—you *won't*. That's always the

problem. There is no command in the Word of God to which we have to answer, "But I can't." God never calls us to an action that He does not enable us to complete. If God says to get rid of something, we can be certain that He will supply the power of the Spirit that will enable us to do the job.

Make no mistake. When we wallow in bitterness, resentment, and self-pity, we make a prison for ourselves. We cannot lay the blame at God's feet. Joseph was a shining example of one who did not allow those emotions to flourish.

Protected for a Unique Purpose

Joseph had the sense that God was at work in his life preparing him for a special task yet to come.

Joseph's body might have been chained, but his spirit was free. Somehow or another, I think Joseph realized that his dreams plus the disaster that had befallen him were leading somewhere. He was determined not to waste this trial.

JOSEPH WAS PROSPERED

Joseph was not only protected, but God prospered him in his captivity. We read the straightforward report, "The Lord was with Joseph and he prospered" (Genesis 39:2).

His Character Was Intact

That's wonderful. Any of us would love to have that written about us. But finish reading the verse: "And [Joseph] lived in the house of his Egyptian master." God put Joseph into a position as a slave because He had lessons for His servant to learn and discoveries for him to make that could not have come his way under any other circumstance.

Joseph had lost his coat but not his character. If all he had going for him was a fancy coat, then he would have been finished when the coat was torn from him. But there was character inside that coat—and God was going to refine and shape that character in the crucible of Egypt.

He Decided to Make the Most of His Situation

Because Joseph was a young man of godly character, somewhere along the line he must have made the decision we talked about at the beginning of the chapter. He must have sat down and said to himself, *I'm going to make the most of this. That's what God wants me to do, and He will enable me to do it.*

I want to suggest that the day Joseph made this decision was the day of his liberation. And the same is true for us. When we can look around at the place where God has put us and say, despite the difficulties, "I'm going to make the most of this for God's glory," we are free.

When Joseph made that decision, it impacted everything he did. He refused to do what would be expected of a captive in a foreign country, which is to do only the minimum necessary to get by. Joseph didn't go around saying, "Sorry, me no speak Egyptian. Can't understand what you're saying. Don't know what you want."

Joseph must have reasoned, *Everyone thinks I'm Potiphar's slave. But I'm actually God's slave. And since I am God's slave, serving Potiphar, I'm going to be the best slave Potiphar ever had.*

There is a lesson here we need to see. Joseph's witness was not in protesting the paganism of Egypt or trying to reorient the culture in which he lived. Those options were not available to him. The only opportunity he had for witness was to be a good slave.

Of course, there are times when protest must be made. And Christians must have a voice in shaping the culture. But for most of us, the real opportunity to impact our world comes when we decide to be the most diligent, obedient, reliable, industrious, and conscientious servants we can be where God has placed us. That's the commitment Potiphar received from Joseph.

God's Blessing Was on Joseph

Notice also that Joseph didn't have to tell Potiphar there was blessing on his life. "[Potiphar] *saw* that the Lord was with him and that the Lord gave him success in everything he did" (Genesis 39:3, italics added).

Potiphar found himself saying, "You know, there's something about this Hebrew kid we picked up in the market. I've had many slaves, but this young man is something special." Oh, to be that kind of person in the marketplace of life!

The favor of God rested on Joseph. When God's blessing is on your life, you won't have to telegraph the news. It will be apparent—even, as in Potiphar's case, to the pagans.

I came across four lines that express this point succinctly and well: "It isn't the style or the stuff in the coat, nor is it the length of the tailor's bill. It's the stuff in the chap inside of the coat that counts for good or ill."

We can dress up like Joseph or wear a hairy shirt like John the Baptist. We can even try to look like Jesus. But we cannot speak with God's authority without the hand of God upon us. Some Christians are in danger of relying on the multicolored coat, as it were, and missing the fact that it's the person inside the coat that really counts.

Are you making the most of your days? Someone may say, "Well, I don't really want to be single. I was hoping to be married by this time."

I understand. But are you making the most of your singleness in the meantime? Are we marrieds making the most of our marriages? Are all of us making the most of every opportunity for God's glory (see Ephesians 5:15–17)?

A fable is told of two grasshoppers that were thrown into a pail of milk. The first grasshopper began immediately to sulk and give up, and he drowned in the milk.

But the second grasshopper began to kick like crazy and work hard at getting out of the pail. In the process, he churned the milk into butter—and then walked out of the pail on top of that block of butter.

Put two people in the same jail cell and one will see only the bars on the window while the other will see the stars beyond the bars. Which would you see?

John Bunyan spent twelve years in a jail in Bedford, England. He was in jail because he refused to preach according to the rules of the day. He wasn't a Church of England clergyman, but he loved to preach.

So the authorities told him, "Bunyan, cut it out or we'll put you in jail."

Bunyan answered, "I can't 'cut it out.' I have to preach." And he preached everywhere he went. So they arrested and jailed John Bunyan, and he languished in his cell for twelve years.

Now, those were rotten circumstances. But within a short time, we are told, there was music coming from Bunyan's cell. He had taken one of the legs of his three-legged stool and carved it into a flute.

John Bunyan did something else in his cell. He wrote *The Pilgrim's Progress*, a book that has become *the* classic after the Bible in the history of Christianity. Millions have been impacted by a work written in the worst of circumstances by a forgotten prisoner in seventeenth-century England.

Prospering in the Drudgery

Talk about drudgery! There was a lot of drudgery in John Bunyan's daily life, and I'm certain there was drudgery in Joseph's day. There's a certain amount of drudgery in our day, too, no matter what we do.

A white-collar businessman commuting to the office on a beautiful summer day was delayed by a flagman on a road-construction crew. As the businessman drove slowly past the flagman, he thought, *Boy, I wish I could be outdoors on a day like this. I'd love to trade places with that flagman and be out in the fresh air and sunshine.*

But as the businessman drove past, the flagman looked at him and thought, *Boy, I wish someone would pay me to sit behind a desk in an air-conditioned office. It's hot out here, and this job is boring. I'd sure like to trade places with that guy today.*

All of us have routine and drudgery. That's why there is no

point in trying to find fulfillment in becoming prosperous enough to escape the routine; there is no escape.

Obviously, we all need downtimes and time away. But the most successful people I've seen are the ones who are able to see the shining blessing of God in the routine experiences of life.

The sixteenth-century writer George Herbert composed the poem "The Elixir," which deals with this subject so well that it became a hymn in Great Britain. Herbert wrote,

> Teach me, my God and King,
> In all things Thee to see,
> And what I do in anything
> To do it as for Thee.
>
> A servant with this clause
> Makes drudgery divine;
> Who sweeps a room as for Thy laws,
> Makes that and the action fine.

Our preoccupation with leisure has led to a mind-set that says, "It's Monday morning, and that's bad. But Friday afternoon is coming, and that's good. So I've got to drag myself through this drudgery until the weekend."

Instead of this, what we need is somebody to remind us, "Do you realize that you were created for God's pleasure? Do you understand that you were made to bring Him glory? This means that every matter you deal with, every moment you spend, every move you make, is an opportunity to bring glory and praise to God." Joseph understood this, and even in slavery he found prosperity.

JOSEPH WAS PROMOTED

This one is hardly surprising. Potiphar did his annual review of his slaves, and this was the result: "Joseph found favor in his eyes and became his attendant. Potiphar put him in charge of his household, and he entrusted to his care everything he owned" (v. 4).

Potiphar's Household Manager

In the same way that Joseph didn't need to tell Potiphar that the Lord was with him, so also he didn't need to ask favors from his master. Joseph was *granted* favor by Potiphar.

George Lawson says, "When men are precious in God's sight, they are honorable, whatever be their station in life. It is good to have those for our friends and for our servants who are beloved by the Lord. His kindness towards His people overflows to all with whom they are connected."

This is exactly what happened in Potiphar's house. A person of his prominent status would look for someone to whom he could delegate the day-to-day details of his household.

Indeed, archaeologists have found that the inscriptions on the tombs of prominent Egyptians also include some reference to the person's steward or attendant because that individual was vital in the life of his master.

That is the kind of steward Joseph became. Potiphar realized he had a good servant, so he expressed his confidence in this young man. And Potiphar was delighted to do so, for the more he delegated to Joseph, the greater was Potiphar's blessing (v. 5).

Why? Because God had determined, for His sovereign purpose, that He would take Joseph to Egypt and protect, prosper, and promote him there. God's hand was upon him, and the blessing spilled over to those who were around him, even the pagans.

This is the only explanation for what was happening in Potiphar's house and his fields. His investment portfolio was going through the roof, and his fields were producing as never before. Potiphar was being made to see what could happen with a life given over to God. It opened the possibility for Potiphar to sit down with Joseph and say, "Can you explain this to me?"

That's the way it's supposed to work. "Let your light shine before men, that they may see your good deeds and praise your Father in heaven" (Matthew 5:16). When men see, they will ask. When they don't see, there's nothing to ask.

The Dangers of Promotion

The roller coaster of Joseph's life has plunged to the bottom of a cistern, risen to the back of a camel, plunged again into Egypt, and now risen to an honored position in Potiphar's house.

But with the increase in his responsibility came a special vulnerability. For the challenge Joseph was now to face was arguably at least as severe as the problems he had faced in the pit in Canaan. Indeed, each spot had its peculiar challenges.

Everyone thinks the next rung up the ladder is *the* spot to be. We think, *If I were to become president of this company, if I were to be chairman of the board, I would do this and that and have no more of this and that*—and we think it would be super.

The people I have spoken with who hold those higher rungs live with a unique vulnerability. There is the dreadful, corrosive effect of carping criticism and the temptation to believe that you're really as good as your position suggests. And then there is the fact that once you have "arrived," people set their eyes on you and your position for all sorts of selfish reasons. Joseph experienced this after his promotion by Potiphar, which was really a promotion from the Lord.

Joseph was now the buzz of the house. He was good-looking and smart and powerful and respectful. Everybody had a good word to say about Joseph.

So we read, "Joseph was well-built and handsome, and after a while his master's wife took notice of Joseph and said, 'Come to bed with me.' But he refused" (Genesis 39:6–8).

Who's to say which location was harder for Joseph? Was it in the cistern where he faced the prospect of death, or was it in the house where he faced temptation?

Here, again, Joseph's story reminds us that when we shun trials, we miss blessings. When all you have is sunshine, all you get is a desert. For most of us, most of the time, it is true that more spiritual progress is made through failure and tears than is made through success and laughter.

A poet penned these well-known words, "I walked a mile with pleasure and she chattered all the way, but left me none the wiser for all she had to say. I walked a mile with sorrow and ne'er a word said she, but oh the things I learned from her, when sorrow walked with me."

It's not that we need to go out and seek sorrowful circumstances so that God can bless us. But when such circumstances come our way, we do well to recognize that in all the pain of human experience and relationships, God is working for our good and His glory, according to the promise of His Word: "We know that in all things God works for the good of those who love him, who have been called according to his purpose" (Romans 8:28).

So we dare not try to manipulate the hand of God. Nor stay awake at night trying to make it all work out for our good. If we belong to Him and have committed our lives to Him, God is at work on our behalf! In believing this we may learn to view difficulties and disappointments, not as stumbling blocks but rather as stepping stones along the path of God's providential care.

Chapter Five

A
POWERFUL
RESPONSE TO
TEMPTATION

The account of Joseph and the lustful advances of Potiphar's wife sounds as though it was taken from yesterday's newspaper or last night's prime-time television program. It has an immediate and striking relevance in that it deals with issues that confront all of us.

But there is an equally striking difference between this story and the sorry sagas of many modern-day celebrities and leaders—namely, the way it ends. Joseph dealt with the advances of Mrs. Potiphar the same way he dealt with the temptation to bitterness or self-pity. He faced it head-on and emerged victorious in the power of God.

Temptation is an enticement to evil or to sin. It is something all of us face, even the Lord Jesus Himself (Matthew 4:1–11). Therefore, it is not a sin to be tempted. It is our response to temptation that leads us down the path of righteousness or into the dead end of disobedience.

We have long ago determined that Joseph was set down in Egypt and in Potiphar's house by the hand of God. God knew that this temptation lay in Joseph's path. And although God did not cause it, since He is never the source of temptation (James 1:13), this incident became part of God's sovereign plan to bring about good in Joseph's life and the lives of his family. A number of factors stand out as we review the powerful and persistent temptation Joseph endured.

THE PECULIAR PERILS OF BEAUTY

We read that "Joseph was well-built and handsome" (Genesis 39:6). So he was vulnerable to the perils that come to the beautiful people of this world.

Joseph was always someone's favorite. He was Jacob's favorite back at home, and he became Potiphar's favorite. And, by reason of his attractiveness, he became the favorite of Potiphar's wife.

Apparently ancient Egypt was no different from America when it came to preferences. Special doors of opportunity swung open for the beautiful people.

Physical attractiveness—beauty of feature or physique—is something a lot of us would like to experience. I can remember coming to the United States as a twenty-year-old in 1972 and being confronted by all those young American men who had haircuts like Marines and bodies that looked as though the men had grown up in a weightlifting room. I was about 147 pounds totally dripping wet, with hair that reached down my back.

I remember feeling distinctly unbeautiful and imagining what it would be like to be one of those handsome guys with the well-sculpted muscles. You may be able to identify with me. We go to the grocery store every week and see the magazines, and they are full of attractive people.

Seeing this, we say to ourselves, *I wonder what it would be like to be one of those people—to look just right all the time, to wear designer clothes, to be handsome of form and face. Wouldn't that be wonderful?*

Our culture suggests that it would be, and many a person is driven by that goal. But human history and the biblical record warn us that the doors that swing open for attractive people can also swing shut and trap them in peril.

Consider the case of Joseph's own great-grandfather, the patriarch Abraham, who had a beautiful wife named Sarah.

As the two were about to enter Egypt to escape a famine in Canaan, Abraham said to Sarah, "I know what a beautiful woman you are. When the Egyptians see you, they will say, 'This is his wife.' Then they will kill me but will let you live. Say you are my sister, so that I will be treated well for your sake and my life will be spared because of you" (Genesis 12:11–13).

Abraham's lie was indefensible, of course, but his fear that the Egyptians would admire Sarah illustrates the peculiar peril of beauty. Joseph faced the same peril. This story would not be in the Bible if he had not been so handsome.

JOSEPH'S POWERFUL TEMPTATION

What are the particulars of this strong temptation? In answering, we get to the heart of the matter. All of us are tempted whether or not we possess beauty. There were at least five elements in the approach Potiphar's wife made toward Joseph.

Her Approach Was Initially Subtle

In Genesis 39:7 the Bible says, "After a while his master's wife took notice of Joseph." This doesn't mean she just said, "Oh, there's Joseph" when she saw him. She "cast her eyes" upon Joseph (KJV). That is, there came a time when she began to notice him. She looked at him, then looked back a second time in a way that was not becoming in a married woman who wants to live in purity.

The eyes are the gateway to the soul, the path through which many loves come. The subtlety of Potiphar's wife was that she began by eyeing Joseph in a lustful way.

Her Approach Was Striking

Once Potiphar's wife had allowed her eyes to ensnare her heart, she completely lost any semblance of modesty. "Come to bed with me!" she proposed to Joseph (v. 7).

How could this woman proceed to such a boldfaced invitation to adultery? The answer is that Potiphar's wife was feeding desire at the level of her imagination. When we do that, we embrace the possibility that we may suddenly do what we've been thinking about.

For example, the advertisement for a certain kind of automobile comes across with such appeal that you imagine yourself, instead of the model, behind the wheel. And suddenly you're behind the wheel—and behind in your payments!

Where did it all start? It started in your imagination. That's where things began with the wife of Joseph's Egyptian master. She fed her lust, and it was ready to break forth in an instant.

Her Approach Was Sustained

Joseph refused the advances of Potiphar's wife (vv. 8–9), but that only served to make him more desirable to her. She kept after him day after day (v. 10), making occasion to be in his company.

She made sure she was there as he came around the corner, then fed him her lines. "Joseph, have you been thinking about me? Come on, Joseph, who's to know? How long has it been since you had a girlfriend? I've been looking for someone like you, Joseph."

Her proposition was clear, but Joseph was equally clear in his answer (we'll deal with his response later). However, this woman was neither corrected by time nor restrained by his refusals.

This tells us something about the danger of allowing oneself to be held in the grip of vain and lustful imagination. It is the trap into which people fall, for example, when they become hooked on pornography.

In their minds, every occasion becomes an occasion for the fulfillment of that lust, and time won't cure the problem. Neither will the refusal of others to become involved. The person becomes enslaved to lust, as Potiphar's wife clearly was.

. Her Approach Was Strategic

When her lustful desire finally got the better of her, Mrs. Potiphar made her move. "One day [Joseph] went into the house to attend to his duties, and none of the household servants was inside" (v. 11).

Bingo. It was the perfect opportunity. Did the woman set this up? There's no one to say. We don't want to make her worse than she actually was. But even if the opportunity just happened to come her way, she took full advantage of it. She figured that as long as no one saw her, it was OK.

Isn't it interesting that when we sin, we think that as long as no one sees us, we're OK? But God sees! And God was Joseph's concern. "How then could I do such a wicked thing and sin against God?" (v. 9). If Joseph's only concern was that no one would find out, this woman's strategic approach at a time when they were alone would have snared him.

When she saw that Joseph wouldn't yield, Potiphar's wife grabbed him. Now I'm sure she didn't just reach out and yank on his coat. The subtleties of a seductress are far more keenly honed than that. She came at him in a way that was most desirable. She laid hold of him in a way that was absolutely compelling. And now he was within the fragrance of her perfume.

This woman traveled down the road from her eyes to her feet to her hands. Through her eyes she imagined what might happen. Then with her feet she put herself in the position to act, and with her hands she expressed her longings.

This is why Jesus said that if our eye causes us to sin, it would be better to pluck it out. Or if our foot or hand causes us to sin, it would be better to cut it off (Mark 9:43–47). The failure to address sin seriously leads us farther down the path.

JOSEPH'S POWERFUL RESISTANCE

There are many things about Joseph that call forth our respect and admiration, and this is one of them: His resistance was as powerful as Mrs. Potiphar's seduction. Notice five features of Joseph's response to this volatile situation as we look at Genesis 39:8–12.

His Resistance Was Decisive

First, we see that Joseph didn't argue with the temptress. Her bold invitation to adultery was met with a decisive refusal (vv. 8–9). We must be just as decisive if we hope to deal with temptation successfully.

We'll have to wait until heaven to be sure, but I firmly believe Joseph had already settled the issue in his mind before the day of crisis came. He could not have helped but notice what archaeological evidence reveals—Egyptian women of that day were notorious for lewdness and immorality.

The pharaohs had a hard time finding a woman who had not been with four or five other men. There is a story in the annals of Egypt of a king who looked for a woman who had been faithful to her husband. Once he found such a woman, he took her away from her husband and made her his wife. That was ancient Egypt.

Joseph could have looked around and decided that a culture like this wasn't so bad after all. But no! Like Daniel, he made up his mind ahead of time that he would not defile himself.

When it comes to temptation, we sow the seeds of our demise when we allow our minds to be uncontrolled. But by guarding our minds, we cultivate our ability to say no.

You cannot make a decision like Joseph's in the heat of the moment. The only way to deal with it is to plan your answer in the cold light of dawn. Joseph was decisive in his refusal.

His Resistance Was Principled

Joseph's response was also based on principle.

He told Potiphar's wife, "With me in charge . . . my master does not concern himself with anything in the house; everything he owns he has entrusted to my care. No one is greater in this house than I am. My master has withheld nothing from me except you, because you are his wife" (vv. 8–9). In other words, there was a rightness about his refusal.

Notice this about Joseph's answer: A lesser individual might have used the same circumstances as an occasion for sin. In other words, someone other than Joseph might have said, "This is perfect. The circumstances are moving me in this direction."

No, circumstances are neutral. Ultimately it is our response to them that makes the difference, and Joseph responded on the basis of principle. "This is not right," he said. "You are Potiphar's wife, and you must fulfill the obligations of being a wife. I am a single man, and I must never intrude upon the privileges of your marriage."

And then, at the end of verse 9, we read that Joseph gave his bottom-line statement, which we quoted earlier. He realized that sin is, in the final analysis, an offense against God.

There is no more powerful force in overcoming temptation than the fear of God. "The fear of the Lord is the beginning of wisdom" (Proverbs 9:10). This is not the servile fear of God that is the fear of a pagan. This is not the fear of what God will do to me, but the fear of what I, by my actions, will do to Him—the fear of dragging down the family name. Joseph feared God.

We are breeding a generation, even in the church, that gives short shrift to the notion of fearing God. "We don't like to think of God in that way anymore. That's a negative image of God. We want to make our message attractive and upbeat."

Fine, let's go ahead and be attractive and upbeat. And meanwhile immorality is rampant inside and outside the church because we are letting go of the foundational principle that stands against immorality, which is the fear of God.

Don't miss the importance of what was happening here. First, Joseph did not address the issue of his desires. The woman was no doubt very beautiful. It's not as though she were repulsive and he didn't feel any attraction for her. That was not the issue.

Neither was the issue that committing adultery would hurt them, or the fact that the news might get out, or any other pragmatic consideration. The issue was that adultery with her would have been an act of wickedness against God.

No matter what contemporary culture says, sexual sin is not just between consenting adults. It is an act of disobedience against God. That's why we don't engage in sexual sin.

This is not just the pragmatic question of what the results might be. Sexual sin is a wicked thing against God, even if every circumstance moves us in that direction. When a culture fails to acknowledge this fact, it condemns itself and trembles on the brink of collapse.

His Resistance Was Unyielding

Joseph's resistance to the advances of his master's wife was also unyielding in its character. It had to be, for "she spoke to Joseph day after day" (v. 10).

It's one thing to resist temptation in its first attack. It's quite another to ratify the decision on a daily basis. Some of us manage to muster enough strength and courage to get past the first temptation, and we're so proud of ourselves for not having yielded that we go right ahead and yield the next time.

Let me give you a trivial example. My church family knows that I have a real problem with peanuts. They are very tempting to me, but I'm not supposed to be eating them.

So I can spend the early part of an evening having a royal war in my mind. I know where the peanuts are, I can see the picture on the can, and I can hear that *pffft!* sound the can makes when you pop the metal seal.

Finally, by about 9:30 P.M., I find myself reasoning as follows: *Alistair, you fought the battle and you won. Man, that's great. I feel so good, I think I'll have a few peanuts to congratulate myself.*

That's a small example, but I've seen plenty of big ones. I have talked to young, unmarried couples who tell me, "Oh, no, Pastor, we don't sleep together. We go here and there, and we keep on the go. We've got it under control."

But a few weeks later, they are skulking around, avoiding

me. I know what happened. The couple used up all their energy saying no once, but they couldn't put their resistance into practice on a daily basis.

Joseph knew it was wrong to give in to Potiphar's wife. He didn't play mind games like the people who say, "You know, Pastor, I fully believe that if God did not want me to enter into this relationship, He would remove the temptation. He would take away the feelings. He would make it clear to me."

The answer is that He has written a whole jolly Book on the subject for you! And He is almost certainly not going to remove the temptation. God is very serious about these issues.

Paul confronted the immorality of the church in Corinth, telling them in no uncertain terms, "You Corinthians are playing fast and loose with the Lord's Supper, and that's why some of you have died" (see 1 Corinthians 11:20–30).

We can't fool with God's requirements. Let's not allow our desires to overturn our reason. We must recognize that the battle is within us, not just outside of us.

We may think we merely respond to the outward temptations that are presented to us. But the truth is that the evil desires in our hearts are constantly searching out temptations to satisfy our lusts. As long as we live in this body, we will wage war against the flesh.

The Westminster Confession says, "We live with a continual and irreconcilable war." Paul says that if we sow the seeds of our lives to please our sinful nature, we will reap destruction. But if we sow to the Spirit, from the Spirit we will reap eternal life (see Galatians 6:8).

Every day we live, we have this choice. Every day we move either in the realm of obedience or the realm of disobedience. There is a propensity within us, even as Christians, to seek out that which is most attractive to us.

The attractions of the world, represented by Potiphar's wife, were brought to Joseph by the Evil One. Would Joseph sow to his flesh and reap destruction, or would he sow to the

Spirit and reap eternal life? God empowered Joseph to make the right choice.

His Resistance Was Physical

Joseph made another wise decision when he refused to be with the woman who was tempting him (v. 10). He avoided her physical presence. He wasn't going to risk the possibility of changing his mind.

You see, Joseph didn't assume that because he had been successful in resisting her on Friday, he would automatically be successful on Saturday. He wasn't so foolish as to say, "I've got this thing licked. It won't bother me."

That's what people tell me all the time. "Don't worry about me, Pastor. I've got it taken care of." Beware if you think that. "If you think you are standing firm, be careful that you don't fall!" (1 Corinthians 10:12).

A Chinese proverb says, "He who would not enter the room of sin must not sit at the door of temptation." Joseph absented himself from the places where he knew Mrs. Potiphar lurked.

His Resistance Was Ruthless

Finally, Joseph was absolutely ruthless in his resistance to the powerful temptation before him.

We read in Genesis 39:12 that when Potiphar's wife grabbed his cloak, he left it in her hand and ran out of the house. Better to lose his cloak than his character. It can take thirty years to build a reputation and only five minutes to ruin it.

That is why Paul told Timothy, "Flee the evil desires of youth" (2 Timothy 2:22). That is why he told the Corinthians, "Flee from sexual immorality" (1 Corinthians 6:18). Don't hang around and play with sexual temptation.

Why? Because, as the writer of Proverbs told his son, "At the end of your life you will groan, when your flesh and body are spent. You will say, 'How I hated discipline! How my heart spurned correction! I would not obey my teachers or listen to my instructors. I have come to the brink of utter ruin in the midst of the whole assembly'" (Proverbs 5:11–14).

How does a young man avoid this miserable end to life? The answer is found in the next section of Proverbs 5, verses 15–20. Let me give these to you as your reading assignment at the end of this section. The summary of the matter is that Joseph's resistance was as powerful as his temptation.

POWERFUL WAYS TO DEAL WITH TEMPTATION

James provides us with powerful principles for applying the truths we have learned here from the life of Joseph. James 1:13–15 is a classic passage on temptation in which the apostle writes, "When tempted, no one should say, 'God is tempting me'" (v. 13).

Temptation Is Not from God

Here's the first principle. God is never, *ever* the source of temptation, as we said at the outset of this chapter. So we can't lay the problem at His feet if we fail.

After Joseph fled from Potiphar's wife, she tried to lay the blame for her lust first at Joseph's feet, and then at the feet of her husband (Genesis 39:13–18). She told the other servants Joseph had tried to rape her, and then she insinuated to Potiphar that it was his fault for bringing Joseph into their home.

Neither of those accusations was true, but when people are under the gun and on the spot, they'll reach for anything to justify themselves. They'll blame others, and they may even try to blame God.

But James says, "God cannot be tempted by evil, nor does he tempt anyone" (James 1:13). God tests us, but the difference between God's testings and the devil's temptations is this: God sets up His tests for His students to *pass*. The temptations of the devil are set up so that his students will *fail*. God is never the author of temptation, so we'll have to place the blame elsewhere.

Temptation Comes from Within

A second principle is that temptation begins with our individual desire. "Each one is tempted when, by his own evil desire, he is dragged away and enticed. Then, after desire has conceived, it gives birth to sin; and sin, when it is full-grown, gives birth to death" (James 1:14–15).

The picture I have in my mind here is that of a hook with bait on it. The mother fish warns her babies not to be tempted by the worm they see dangling in the water, for if they bite into it they are going to be supper for the fisherman.

But little Freddie Fish decides his mother is getting old and losing it, so he decides to take a bite of the worm. The hook grabs him, and he's history.

Now that may be a silly illustration, but it conveys the idea. We get ourselves hooked by sin because we want the worm.

Temptation Demands the Right Response

God's Word promises us that we will never face a temptation for which He does not provide an exit, an escape route, "so that [we] can stand up under it" (1 Corinthians 10:13).

Now this is not a promise we can apply passively. It's a promise of power to escape and overcome any temptation, but we still have to look for the exit. We need to deal decisively with temptation. I find it helpful to have five words in mind as I think about tackling temptation.

1. Deal with temptation *immediately*. Don't wait until the little stream becomes a raging river that will sweep you away. The moment we become conscious of any sinful thought or desire, we need to ask God to help us reject the suggestion and dismiss it.

2. Deal with temptation *realistically*. God told Cain, "Sin is crouching at your door; it desires to have you" (Genesis 4:7). If there is a lion on the other side of the door waiting to pounce on you, you'd better get realistic about

the situation before you blithely open the door. Jesus said to His disciples, "Watch and pray so that you will not fall into temptation" (Matthew 26:41).

3. Deal with temptation *ruthlessly*. I would remind you here of Jesus' graphic metaphors for dealing with sin (Mark 9:43–48). In the Falkland's War, Margaret Thatcher ordered the bombing of the British runway in Port Stanley so as to prevent enemy aircraft from landing. That serves as a useful analogy.

4. Deal with temptation *consistently*. Establish patterns of resistance.

A sailor on the south coast of England told his chaplain, "Chaplain, you don't understand. You're telling us to walk the straight and narrow path. But you don't realize the temptations we face, the way we're blown and tossed about. We can't really be blamed for what happens to us."

The chaplain drew the sailor's attention to the water, where two sailboats were moving along with their sails flapping in the wind. One was heading west, the other east. The chaplain said, "One boat goes east, one boat goes west. By the self-same winds that blow. It's the set of their sails and not the gales, that determine which way they go."

Do we have our sails set in the direction of obedience to God? If so, we can go the right way, even if the whole world is blown off course. Joseph had set his sails long before Potiphar's wife tried to steer his life onto the rocks.

5. Deal with temptation *confidently*. The promise of 1 Corinthians 10:13 gives us an unshakable confidence in facing temptation because its terms are absolute.

Remember those old movie Westerns? The cowboys would be trapped in a canyon with the Indians all around them, and it looked like curtains. But then some guy with a cigar stump in his mouth and stubble on his face would say, "Follow me. I have found a way to safety." And off they would go.

Be honest. Did you ever give in to temptation because there was no way of escape? You never did, and neither did I. God *always* has a way out. The problem comes when we close our eyes to the escape route because we have allowed our desires to overwhelm our reason.

A WORD OF HOPE

If talking about temptation is a painful experience for you because of mistakes and failures in your past, let me leave you with a word of hope.

Martin Luther says, "Our Lord speaks with sweet reasonableness." It's never too late for repentance. With God's help we can chart a new course and set our sails in the direction of obedience to God. The Lord says, "I will forgive [your] wickedness and will remember [your] sins no more" (Jeremiah 31:34).

God's word to you is the same word Jesus gave to the woman caught in adultery (John 8:1–11). After all her pharisaic accusers had slunk away one at a time, Jesus asked her, "Has no one condemned you?" When the woman answered, "No one, sir," Jesus said to her, "Then neither do I condemn you. . . . Go now and leave your life of sin."

No matter what has happened, you can leave your life of sin by the enabling of the Spirit of God through the Word of God. His power to overcome temptation is available to us all.

Chapter Six

ℬACK IN THE HOLE AGAIN

The hand of God has just been lifted up in deliverance. Joseph has experienced what the psalmist describes: "This poor man called, and the Lord heard him; he saved him out of all his troubles" (Psalm 34:6).

Potiphar's wife's attempts at seduction had failed. Joseph had lost his cloak but not his character. He had kept his purity, but was about to lose his position. He had previously been dumped into a cistern by his brothers, and now he was about to be thrown into a dungeon by his boss. Having had the run of Potiphar's house, he was now being run out of the house! The one who had been in charge was now being charged with a terrible crime.

THE ACTIONS OF POTIPHAR AND HIS WIFE

As we have said, we have a pretty good inkling of what Potiphar's wife was like. She didn't hesitate to lie about her encounter with Joseph, and unfortunately Potiphar believed her. That's how Joseph wound up in an Egyptian dungeon (Genesis 39:19–20).

Joseph himself referred to his prison as a dungeon (40:15). There can be little doubt that it was a dreadful and sunless hole. I've been in a few dungeons in castles throughout the United

Kingdom. They are deep and cramped and devoid of a significant supply of oxygen, certainly not the kind of place you
would want to spend a great deal of time.

So let's not get the idea that Joseph moved from a nice
room to a not-so-nice room. His new "home" was not designed
for the care of the prisoners. The most common sound was the
relentless clanging of chains.

Prisoners in dungeons were manacled, and the chain fastened to a central pillar. Any movement was defined by the
length of the chain.

Years later, the psalmist referred to Joseph's imprisonment.
"They bruised his feet with shackles, his neck was put in irons,
till what he foretold came to pass, till the word of the Lord
proved him true" (Psalm 105:18–19).

With irons on his feet and neck, it would have been difficult for Joseph even to raise his head and look up, much less
move. There is a symmetry to Genesis 39, for just as Joseph
had arrived in Egypt in chains, so now he was again in chains,
albeit in a different location.

The Treachery of Potiphar's Wife

This latest downward turn in Joseph's life began at the
hands of the woman who would have surely been on the society pages in Egypt, if they had had such a thing. Mrs. Potiphar
had prestige and position. She was one of the beautiful people,
yet her life was in absolute shambles.

This woman was like so many people in contemporary culture. She looked good on the outside. She had it all; she was
nicely put together. If you saw her you would assume she had
everything going for her.

But she didn't. She was a walking disaster zone. The wife of
Potiphar was surrounded by many gods, but she didn't know
the God of Joseph. She believed a fine perfume was more pres-
tigious than a fine name. She had health, possessions, and influence but lacked the ability to enjoy them.

Mrs. Potiphar would doubtless have concurred with legendary actress Sophia Loren, who said some time ago, "In my life there is an emptiness it is impossible for me to fill." Potiphar's wife had a lot, but it was the wrong stuff. If we'd seen her in the mall we might have envied her, but her glamorous façade was a thin disguise for her flawed character.

First of all, she had an adulterous heart. She was consumed with lust, and she was on the prowl. It would be surprising if Joseph was the only man she had ever attempted to seduce in the course of her marriage.

Second, because of her consuming lust, the wife of Joseph's master could not bear to have her evil desires unfulfilled. She was used to getting what she wanted. Indeed, she was prepared to go to almost any length to get what she desired, and her failure to do so drove her to the worst of actions in respect to Joseph.

Third, Potiphar's wife was an able liar. She made lies her refuge (see Isaiah 28:15). As we saw in the previous chapter, as soon as events went against her wishes she resorted to her refuge. She lied about the whole affair even as she gazed straight into the eyes of her husband.

Fourth, she was capable of murderous hatred. I say that because instead of being imprisoned, Joseph could easily have lost his head. That would have been the expected penalty for a slave who was accused of assaulting the master's wife. Mrs. Potiphar's approach was, "If I can't have him, I'll make sure nobody else gets him."

Fifth, and finally, she was a skillful manipulator. As we saw in the last chapter, she insinuated that Potiphar was at fault for what had happened. "That Hebrew slave you brought us came to me to make sport of me," she told her husband (v. 17).

In other words, "This is all your fault, Potiphar. If you hadn't bought this slave, this wouldn't have happened to me." Then, in verse 19, we read that she said, "This is how *your* slave treated me" (italics added).

Taken together, this is quite a personality. Potiphar's wife did her evil then stepped off the scene. But Joseph was caught in the wreckage she left behind.

Potiphar's Rage and Bad Decision

Potiphar is the third person on center stage in this drama of God's providence in the life of Joseph.

Potiphar was obviously a masterful delegator and a shrewd judge of character. He could pick out a good slave. He was able to determine that Joseph had something special about him. And it is hardly surprising that Potiphar reacted in anger at the thought that his most trusted slave had tried to steal his wife's purity.

Any husband worth his salt must react in this way. Even the very idea that his wife's purity has been threatened is abhorrent to a man, especially if the culprit is someone he has brought into the household. So Potiphar's reaction is understandable. There is a rightness about that sort of protection.

But shouldn't Potiphar have stepped back for a moment to consider his wife's story? We know he should have, but apart from our perspective there are several features of his wife's account that should have given Potiphar reason to proceed slowly in judging Joseph. After all, as captain of the king's guard, Potiphar was used to investigating all sorts of allegations.

First, he should have realized that it would have been stupid of Joseph to leave behind such damaging evidence as his cloak if he were truly guilty. Potiphar's wife was not as strong as Joseph, so why hadn't Joseph grabbed the incriminating garment from her when he ran? Joseph had to know that as a slave, his life was as good as over if the charge against him were to be proven.

A second inconsistency in her story was the record of Joseph's faithful service in the household. Years had passed since he had arrived. Joseph was twenty-seven years old by the close of Genesis 39. Joseph's record should have earned him at least some benefit of the doubt.

But Potiphar would hear none of it. He allowed his anger to do away with his judgment. We read, "He burned with anger" (v. 19). He was enraged, and in that frame of mind he was incapable of hearing either truth or reason. The result was that he made a bad decision, the same as we do the majority of the time when we make decisions in anger.

If you listen to the Word of God with an angry heart, you will hear the pastor talking but you will *not* hear the Word of God to your spirit. That's why people can sit under the ministry of the Word, and yet it rolls off them like water off a slate roof.

Anger will always blind the mind. That's why James writes, "Man's anger does not bring about the righteous life that God desires" (James 1:20). Better to take a long walk in the rain and get soaking wet than to let anger rule your spirit.

There's a second reason Potiphar summarily imprisoned Joseph. He allowed himself to be unduly influenced by his wife.

Now I didn't say simply that Potiphar allowed himself to be influenced by his wife. I said *unduly* influenced. That is the key word. Every man is influenced by his wife—and in most cases, mercifully and gratefully so. But we men are not to be unduly influenced by our wives. To the man falls the responsibility of leadership and the headship of the home.

There is no doubt that Potiphar's wife had a pretty good tongue in her head. She was adept at intimidating her husband. It's been my observation that many an apparently powerful leader is led around by his nose when he goes home.

Listen to John Calvin. "Husbands are especially taught that they must use prudence, lest they should be carried rashly hither and thither at the will of their wives." This is not politically correct, but it is biblically accurate.

The commentator George Lawson says, "Potiphar paid too much deference to his wife. He ought not to have believed her words against Joseph without examining the truth of them. A man ought to love his wife as a part of himself, but however dear she may be to him, truth and justice ought to be still dearer."

And so, under the influence of rage and goaded by his wife's intimidation, Potiphar assigned his faithful Hebrew slave to "the place where the king's prisoners were confined" (Genesis 39:20). Without conducting a thorough investigation and without allowing Joseph to mount a defense, Potiphar dealt Joseph a swift and dreadful blow that may have plunged a lesser individual into despair.

THE PERSPECTIVE OF JOSEPH

This godly young man was back in the hole again. Humanly speaking, this poor fellow's life was either moving full speed ahead or grinding to a dead stop. There was little middle ground.

The Price He Paid for Principle

As the warden of the dungeon put the shackles around Joseph's ankles and the iron around his neck, what do you think was going through Joseph's mind?

Was there at least the fleeting notion, *Is this what I get for doing it right? Is this the reward for integrity? Maybe I'm missing something here.*

These thoughts may have raced through his mind, but I believe that, somehow, Joseph knew better than this. Recall that he had made his response to Potiphar's wife not on the basis of pragmatism, but on the strength of principle.

It wasn't only that adultery would hurt the people involved, or that it was intrinsically a bad idea, or that they might get caught. The issue for Joseph was "How then could I do such a wicked thing and sin against God?" (v. 9).

This is the thing that will keep us on the narrow way. Jerry Bridges says, "The narrow way was never hit upon by chance, neither did a heedless man ever live a holy life." What keeps a man or woman true to the Lord is not pragmatism, but principle.

Joseph had reasoned in his heart concerning the seductions

of Potiphar's wife, *If this comes my way, this is what I will do—and whatever happens, so be it.* Now it had happened, and he was in a horrible pigsty of a dungeon.

And, yet, look at him. The object of the undeserved hatred of his brothers and the subject of untrue accusations by Potiphar's wife; the bottom had dropped out of his world—and yet his attitude of patient endurance remained. Whether a household manager or a prisoner, Joseph was the same person. He was a man of principle.

THE FAVOR HE FOUND IN THE DUNGEON

Even in this extremity, our man became the object of God's favor. "When a man's ways are pleasing to the Lord, he makes even his enemies live at peace with him" (Proverbs 16:7). In the worst of circumstances God can raise up friends for His servants:

> *While Joseph was there in prison, the Lord was with him; he showed him kindness and granted him favor in the eyes of the prison warden. So the warden put Joseph in charge of all those held in the prison, and he was made responsible for all that was done there. The warden paid no attention to anything under Joseph's care, because the Lord was with Joseph and gave him success in whatever he did.* (Genesis 39:20–23)

In a change of jobs, a change of schools, or some other change of circumstance, most of us have known that lonely feeling of being by ourselves, of not having anyone around who can even remotely be considered a friend. This is especially painful for a student at a new school, and I speak from personal experience. In the middle of all that you say, "I wonder if I'll ever have another friend again." But, then, from the most unlikely quarters, God raises up a friend for you. He did so for Joseph.

THE HEART OF GOD'S PROMISE

Let's push the pause button on the video of Joseph's life for just a moment. We need to notice something important about the promise God gives us in Romans 8:28, the verse that is our foundation for this book.

The truth of Romans 8:28 is far more than just what I call kitchen-verse theology. Now let me explain what I mean by that.

Kitchen-verse theology is when we take a plaque with a verse on it and stick it above the kitchen sink, with the idea that when we say it over and over again as a sort of Christian mantra, it will somehow start working for us. This is often accompanied by the notion that working for "our good" will mean an abundance of sunshine and the absence of rain. But the idea that Romans 8:28 is only "at work" in the sunshine and not the storm produces a theology of triumphalism.

Such a perspective fails to reckon with life when the clouds come and the wheels fall off. We need to learn that God's providential hand is at work in the hard times. And that He works for the good of those who love Him in *all* things—not just in the triumphs and successes, but in the dungeon. The "good" of those who love Him is ultimately our conformity to Christ and our sanctification.

We need also to recognize that when God in His providence shines His light into our darkness, as He did in the dungeon for Joseph, He's not doing it because we have merited His favor. You see, some of us have got it right about the doctrine of justification. We understand that we cannot earn salvation, which is a gift of God's free grace. But that's true not only of *coming to* Christ, but also of *living for* Christ. We don't merit His favor. He doesn't repay us for the good things we've done by making the sun shine on us. If Joseph had anticipated that, how would we explain what happened to him?

Joseph responded to temptation with absolute integrity and purity, and what was his reward? A trip to the dungeon. But then, suddenly, in the midst of that experience, the clouds parted and the sun shone upon him in the person of the warden.

God chose to do this out of His own goodness, motivated

by nothing in Joseph and driven by nothing in the circumstances, but only by His sovereign plan and purpose. John
Calvin says, "Since we are unworthy that He should grant us
his help, the cause of its communication must be in Himself,
seeing that He is merciful."

Some of us are still living with a form of cause-and-effect
Christianity. But think about the way we parents love our children. We say no to them in certain things. The kids don't understand, and they complain. But we do it anyway, because it's
for their good.

And sometimes, when they are least deserving, we lavish
our attention upon them so as to move their hearts to repentance at the awareness of our unconditional favor. We do so because we love them with a passion.

God is far more willing to bless us than we are to take the
time to even ask Him for blessings. And when He shines the
sun of His providence into the life of His servant, it is not because the servant has merited God's favor, which is induced by
nothing other than God's goodness.

So when we sing, "God is so good, He's so good to me," we
have to acknowledge that this remains true even in the dungeon—because our good God is working all things out in conformity with the purpose of His will.

Our problem is that we have a limited perspective. All we
can see is Earth, not what God is doing from heaven's side to
bring about His good purpose in us and in others.

If we could see all that God is doing, we would say, "Oh,
this is fabulous!" But, instead, we're tempted to declare, "I don't
think I should be in this dark dungeon. This shouldn't be happening to me. This isn't fair."

That's why we need a theology. We can't live wisely without biblical doctrine. We can live only as silly people.

But once we begin to understand the great truths that un-
derpin our faith, we can say with John Wesley,

Commit thy ways to Him
Thy works into His hands;
And rest in His unchanging Word
Who heaven and earth commands.

Through waves and clouds and storms
His power will clear thy way;
Wait thou His time; the darkest night
Shall end in brightest day.

Leave to His sovereign sway
To choose and to command;
So shalt thou, wondering, own His way
How wise, how strong His hand.

Joseph hadn't read Romans 8:28. He didn't have it hanging on the wall of his dungeon. But he understood the truth behind it, and even in the worst of human circumstances he displayed patient endurance and quiet confidence.

I remember a dear lady I often visited in the hospital in Edinburgh. She had been the chief nurse in the royal infirmary and had given her entire life to the care of others. Now, hospitalized in grave condition, she would say to me, "Alistair, read me the Bible. Just read me the Bible."

This woman knew she had little prospect of being discharged. But she knew where she was going when she left. Joseph had no prospect of coming out of the dungeon. But he knew that God was working in his life for good (Genesis 50:20).

THE RESPONSE OF THE WARDEN

What about the warden of the dungeon, the fourth character in the story?

If you remember those old movies about medieval England with a dungeon under the castle and a hulking figure in charge, you'll know that this man didn't get his job because he was a nice guy. When they interviewed him, they weren't checking his fingernails to see if they were clean, and they weren't testing him to see if he was a people person. "Wanted: Prison warden, good people skills." No, it wasn't like that. All that mattered was how good he was with the ax and the screws. This was a position that called for brutality.

Now if I had been the prison warden and this foreigner Joseph showed up, I wouldn't have been too excited about him. After all, I would have been in Potiphar's employ a lot longer than he, yet he was put in charge of the whole operation. I would have instinctively disliked Joseph. And I would have been delighted to fasten those manacles and irons on him nice and tight.

So as Joseph looked around for friends, he had no reason to expect that the warden would be anything but his enemy.

Yet God had other ideas. The Lord turned the warden's heart toward Joseph.

If we had asked the warden, "What do you make of all of this?" he would have said, "I don't know. In all of my life, I've never met anybody like Joseph. I've never experienced anything like this. I've never seen Potiphar soften the way he softened in relationship to that young man.

"And, frankly, I can't even explain the change in my heart toward Joseph."

THE SOVEREIGN HAND OF GOD

The key, of course, is the hand of God moving among the personalities and particulars of the story. Simply put, the Lord was with Joseph (Genesis 39:21).

Why did Potiphar spare Joseph's life and the warden show favor to Joseph? The answer is that "the king's heart is in the hand of the Lord; he directs it like a watercourse wherever he pleases" (Proverbs 21:1). There is nothing to suggest that Joseph tried to manipulate the circumstances to his own ends. He was the object of God's sovereign care—and so are you.

God's Care for Joseph

As I thought about this, my mind went immediately to Psalm 139, that great psalm which tells of God's attending care over the minutest details of our lives.

I want to paraphrase this psalm by putting it in the Lord's voice rather than the psalmist's, and by addressing it to Joseph, in order to answer the question, What would God say to Joseph in that dungeon? In that setting, Psalm 139 reads like this:

"Joseph, I have searched you and I know you. I know when you sit down and when you stand up. I know your thoughts from afar. I discern your going out and your lying down. I'm familiar with all your ways. Before you say anything, Joseph, I know it completely.

"Joseph, I have hemmed you in, behind and before. I have laid My hand upon you. Where can you go from My spirit? Where can you flee from My presence? If you go up to the heavens, Joseph, I am there. If you make your bed in the depths, I am there. If you rise up on the wings of the dawn, if you settle on the far side of the sea, even there My hand will guide you. My right hand will hold you fast.

"Joseph, if you say, 'Surely the darkness will hide me, and the light will become night around me,' even the darkness will not be dark to Me. The night will shine like the day.

"Joseph, I created you. I knit you together in your mother's womb. You have every reason to praise Me because you are fearfully and wonderfully made.

"Your frame wasn't hidden from Me when I made you in the secret place. I wove you together in the depths of the earth. My eyes saw your unformed body. All the days ordained for you were written in My book before one of them came to be.

"Joseph, the sum of My thoughts toward you is vast; they outnumber the grains of sand."

GOD'S CARE FOR YOU

And if this is true of Joseph, it's also true of you in Christ. I don't know your circumstances. You may feel like you are in a dungeon right now. You may be suffering mistreatment. But the Lord knows. He's not taken by surprise. And He loves you with an everlasting love.

In the mid-1960s there was a horribly violent uprising in the newly independent African nation that had been the colony called the Belgian Congo. Many people, including dozens of missionaries, were brutalized and murdered. Right in the eye of that storm was a group of medical missionaries, including Dr. Helen Roseveare.

She had graduated from Cambridge University and had offered her medical skills to the Lord in His service, saying she wanted to serve Christ no matter where, and no matter what the cost.

Dr. Roseveare went to serve Christ in the Congo, only to find herself in the midst of unbelievable chaos. Before her eyes, some of her colleagues were shot through the temple and dropped into an open grave. She and other young women were brutalized at the hands of the rebel troops. The story is told in Dr. Roseveare's tremendous book, *Give Me This Mountain*.

I was privileged to have met Dr. Roseveare and to have heard her speak. In a letter I received from her, she said, "The phrase God gave me years ago, during the 1964 rebellion in Congo, in the night of my own greatest need, was this: 'Can you thank Me for trusting you with this experience, even if I never tell you why?'" Dr. Roseveare was able to say yes to that question.

What a tremendous challenge! You see, we have no right to demand of God an explanation. He has every right to ask of us genuine consecration.

And as it was with Joseph and Helen Roseveare and so many others, so it was with Jesus Himself. "When they hurled their insults at him, he did not retaliate; when he suffered, he made no threats. Instead, he entrusted himself to him who judges justly" (1 Peter 2:23).

May we follow the example of Joseph—and of Jesus—and place ourselves in the caring, loving hand of God.

A
GAME PLAN
FOR SUFFERING

As we reflect upon the story so far we might be tempted to think that Joseph was almost superhuman.

Joseph's reaction to incredible trials makes most of us feel we are a long way from being the kind of person Joseph was.

But this young Hebrew was human, of course, and we get a glimpse of his human frailty as he pleads with the cupbearer of Pharaoh to speak a good word for him and help him get out of prison. It was clear to him that he had done nothing to deserve his imprisonment (Genesis 40:14–15).

Joseph was not a fatalist. He was not sitting in prison singing, "Whatever will be, will be." He recognized that all of his days and his decisions were under God's providential care. But he also realized that God had given him a mind with which to think, the ability to take initiative, and influence among many people in Egypt.

Joseph's request was simple. When the cupbearer was released, Joseph asked him to "remember me . . . show me kindness . . . mention me to Pharaoh . . . get me out of this prison" (v. 14). But Joseph was treated unjustly again. The cupbearer did not remember Joseph; he forgot him.

What a saga of injustice, and what potential for bitterness. Joseph was opposed, imprisoned, maligned, misunderstood, slandered, falsely accused, and wrongfully persecuted. (Apart from that, everything was fine!) Once again, in the details of his life, Joseph foreshadowed Jesus Christ.

Peter reminds his readers of Jesus: "When they hurled their insults at him, he did not retaliate; when he suffered, he made no threats. Instead, he entrusted himself to him who judges justly" (1 Peter 2:23). Joseph was definitely a type, or foreshadowing, of Christ.

Just like Joseph, we will experience seasons in our lives when we will find ourselves on the receiving end of accusations, slander, and other forms of mistreatment. This is hard to take when it is undeserved. It comes like a hard slap in the face that stuns and surprises us.

But if, indeed, trouble in the form of unjust suffering is sure to come our way—and Jesus says it will (John 16:33)—then we needn't be taken aback by it. Instead, we need to know how to handle it when it comes.

DON'T BE SURPRISED BY SUFFERING

The first thing we need to understand is that suffering is not the unusual exception for the Christian. Therefore, we should not be surprised when we suffer unjustly.

Peter writes to the church, "Dear friends, do not be surprised at the painful trial you are suffering, as though something strange were happening to you" (1 Peter 4:12). Don't be taken off guard by unjust suffering, Peter says, because that is the way Jesus suffered. And when we suffer in the same way, we are actually participating in Jesus' sufferings (v. 13).

No Guarantee Against Suffering

The great temptation for us as Christians is to regard suffering as a strange misfortune, something totally out of step with what following Jesus is all about. After all, doesn't Romans

8:28 promise us that God will bring good out of all the events of our lives?

The problem is often the way we define what is good. Most people think of "the good" as health, security, and prosperity. Anybody harboring that notion of Christian living is going to be surprised by suffering.

How did we arrive at the conclusion that following Christ is a walk in the park? Where did we get the idea that serving Christ is a guarantee against trial and pain and persecution?

We didn't get it from Jesus. He guarantees just the opposite. "In this world you will have trouble" (John 16:33). And in His own life, our Lord was the supreme example of a person who suffered unjustly.

During the trial of Jesus, Pilate said repeatedly, "I find no basis for a charge against him" (John 18:38; 19:4, 6). The Roman governor knew Jesus' enemies had delivered Him up out of jealousy, not because He had done anything wrong. Nevertheless, Pilate had Jesus cruelly flogged (19:1) and then turned Him over to be crucified.

With Jesus' experience in mind, consider the question Peter asks. "How is it to your credit if you receive a beating for doing wrong and endure it? But if you suffer for doing good and you endure it, this is commendable before God" (1 Peter 2:20).

At school in Scotland we were punished with a leather strap. The male teachers carried a belt under their jacket, slung over their shoulder. As kids we always looked for that telltale lump under the teacher's jacket, because that was where he went to pull out his implement of destruction to beat us on the hands as we held them out in front of us.

If a student deserved his punishment, the others didn't think much about it because they understood the reason. But when an injustice was done and an innocent student was strapped, the sense of support and camaraderie in the class was almost palpable.

The punishment Jesus endured was totally unjust—and yet

we are told that His suffering is an example for us, so that we might "follow in his steps" (1 Peter 2:21). Those people listed in the gallery of faith certainly understood this (Hebrews 11:35–38).

So wherever the idea of easy faith came from, it didn't come from Jesus. Nor did it come from Joseph. His life story to this point was nothing but a saga of suffering even though he had committed no evil.

The contemporary American church is too quick to believe that every experience of unjust suffering has to do with believers from a time and place that are far removed from us.

That simply isn't true. Paul says of the apostles, "we have become the scum of the earth, the refuse of the world" (1 Corinthians 4:13). This is what the world really thinks of Christians.

Paul is speaking of himself and his colleagues, the ministers of the gospel, and he says the world treats them the way we treat the stuff we put down our disposals after a meal. Is it a wonder that the Romans could throw Christians to the lions and burn them as torches? You don't worry about disposing of garbage.

Someone has said that Christians are going to be the Jews of the twenty-first century—mistreated, persecuted, and not tolerated. It is not difficult to envisage how that might happen.

The Roman Empire in which Paul lived was a pluralistic culture. Now, let's not get confused by the word *pluralism*. The term doesn't simply mean that all ideas are tolerated and people are free to think whatever they want.

Pluralism is not as benign as that. It is, instead, the theory that the ultimate reality of the universe consists of a plurality of entities. Pluralism says that truth cannot be found in any one dogma or person. Syncretism advances that notion and says it is in the blending of all those entities that we arrive at the truth.

So the Romans practiced pantheism, the worship of a multiplicity of gods. If someone showed up with a new god, the Romans simply moved the others over a bit and made a place for the new god. Religiously, the culture was open to just about any idea.

How was it, then, that in such a religiously diverse and tolerant culture so much unjustified suffering was meted out to Christians? It was because Christians were not prepared to merely add Christ to the pantheon. They worshiped him as the only God.

Christians refused to say that Jesus was just another way to God or another expression of religious reality. They declared with Peter, "There is no other name under heaven given to men by which we must be saved" (Acts 4:12). So too must we.

Insist on that truth in a pluralistic culture like that of Rome, or like that of the modern-day United States, and you will at some point bring suffering upon yourself. Remind people that Jesus Himself says He is the only Way to the Father (John 14:6), and you will encounter hatred and opposition. Don't be surprised by it when it comes.

People will say to you, "That's an arrogant position. Who in the world do you think you are? Where did you Christians get the idea that you have a corner on the truth? How can you be so dogmatic?"

The answer is that if a position is true, to hold it isn't arrogant. And if it isn't true, to hold it is just stupidity. In our post-Christian, pluralistic, and increasingly hostile culture, if we are going to stand for the truth of Christ we had better not be surprised when the painful trial comes upon us.

Now I may be wrong, and in one sense I pray that I am. But as we look toward the horizon, there is every indication that orthodox Christianity, with its insistence on the sufficiency and authority of Scripture and the exclusivity of Christ, will not be tolerated, but instead will be vehemently opposed in the next millennium.

That's because pluralists can only tolerate other pluralists. Pluralists are mercilessly intolerant toward those who refuse to subscribe to their views.

When we declare that Jesus—and Jesus alone—is the Way,

the Truth, and the Life; when people know clearly where we stand; we will become a thorn in the side of a pluralistic, pantheistic world. So, again, don't be surprised when you suffer for being a Christian.

DON'T QUIT WHEN YOU SUFFER

One problem with unjust suffering is the tremendous temptation it brings to throw in the towel, to quit trying to maintain one's integrity and standards of righteousness.

We have noted this several times before, but Joseph is a classic example of someone who, humanly speaking, had every reason to say, "What's the use of trying to be righteous?"

As he sat in that Egyptian dungeon, Joseph could have said, "That's it. I might as well do what everyone else does. I don't see where trying to obey God and maintain my integrity is working to my benefit. I thought I was mistreated before, but now I'm in prison because of a perverse woman. I don't deserve this."

We have no record that Joseph thought these things, but the temptation was certainly there because he was human. You may be tempted to reach the same conclusion. It does seem at times that the rascals who are cheating on their spouses and their taxes are having a great time, while the righteous often wind up in the pit for doing right.

For your encouragement I commend to you Psalm 73: The psalmist makes the same lament but his eyes are opened in a major way when he enters the house of God.

F. B. Meyer says, "Do right because it is right to do right. And when you determine to do right because it is right to do right, then when you're misunderstood, ill-treated, when you're the victim of unjust suffering, you won't swerve, you won't sit down, you won't whine, and you won't despair."

That's the wonderful thing about Joseph. How is it that he didn't whine and despair when his life kept taking a wrong turn? Sure, he wanted to get out of prison. He asked for help in getting out, but he was not whining.

Why? Because he had determined to do the right thing no matter the cost and no matter where it took him.

Hebrews 12:3 is a great antidote for those who feel like quitting. After urging us to fix our eyes on Jesus, the writer says, "Consider him who endured such opposition from sinful men, so that you will not grow weary and lose heart."

Having a hard time? Think of Jesus. Someone maligning you? Think of Jesus. Feeling like throwing in the towel, giving up, losing heart? Consider what Jesus endured. After all, "in your struggle against sin, you have not yet resisted to the point of shedding your blood" (Hebrews 12:4) the way Jesus did. You haven't died yet, the writer of Hebrews says. So don't give up.

DON'T TAKE REVENGE WHEN YOU SUFFER

Ours is the most litigious society in the world. There are more lawsuits here on these fair shores than on any other place on Earth.

One of the reasons is that people are so vengeful. When they suffer wrong at the hands of someone, or even *perceive* that they have suffered wrong, their response to the other person is, "I'll get you in the end." And that's not a love song they're singing.

Overcoming Evil with Good

But as God's people, we are called to an entirely different standard. The apostle Paul tells us how to respond to unjust suffering:

> Do not repay anyone evil for evil. Be careful to do what is right in the eyes of everybody. If it is possible, as far as it depends on you, live at peace with everyone. Do not take revenge, my friends, but leave room for God's wrath, for it is written: "It is mine to avenge; I will repay," says the Lord. On the contrary: "If your enemy is hungry, feed him; if he is thirsty, give him something to drink. In doing this, you will heap burning coals on his head." Do not be overcome by evil, but overcome evil with good. (Romans 12:17–21)

Notice that our first responsibility is to do what is right and to do all we can to maintain peace with others. When the other person refuses to keep the peace, we have a clear course of action set out for us to deal with the offense and restore peace.

Joseph gave us many examples of Romans 12 in action. One is the way he forgave his brothers when he had them in his power as prime minister of Egypt, but that came much later. The occasion I'm thinking of is the way Joseph accepted the responsibility given him in prison (Genesis 39:21–23). He could have sulked and refused to do anything but sit in his cell, grousing about the great injustice he had suffered. Or he could have allowed himself to be overcome by the cumulative weight of the evil done to him and started returning some evil himself. But he chose another course.

One of my children came home one day deeply upset by something that had happened at school. Her reaction was, "I'll never speak to those people again. Or I'll give them a piece of my mind, because I've thought of some good replies to this."

So we sat down, and I said, "Instead, why not write them a note? 'I'm sorry about what happened yesterday. I forgive you. You're my friends.' Then sign your name."

"No way! You weren't there, Dad. You didn't hear it."

"Honey, you can do it your own way if you want, but that's my suggestion."

The following day, I got a call at the office. It was my daughter, and she was excited. "Dad, I did it! I wrote the note. Later, I was in the bathroom and my friends came in crying and said, 'We're sorry.' And we hugged each other and cried for a while. It was fantastic. You were right, Dad."

We may smile at that, but the truth is that our own disputes are just a grown-up version of things that happen in school. When you cut to the heart of it, it's all an extension of the "he said, she said" merry-go-round.

So much of this stuff can be cured or even prevented by refusing to seek revenge for wrongs suffered. When Jesus was reviled, He didn't revile in return. When He suffered, He didn't curse or threaten His tormenters.

Letting God Vindicate Us

Paul says that when we refuse to take our revenge, instead returning evil with good, God becomes our defender (Romans 12:19).

Paul gives us an example from his own life. He was being slandered in Corinth, but his response was to say, "I care very little if I am judged by you or by any human court. . . . My conscience is clear, but that does not make me innocent. It is the Lord who judges me" (1 Corinthians 4:3–4).

It's a great mistake to spend our lives trying to justify ourselves, explain our motives, or get the scrambled eggs back into their shells. Many people will say and think what they want to regardless of what we do, so let's get on with serving God and leave our vindication with Him. He's the One we will answer to and the One we need to please.

The great Scottish reformer and preacher John Knox understood this perfectly. It was said of Knox that he feared the face of God so much that he never feared the face of any man. That was good, because people used to throw stools and pieces of merchandise at Knox when he preached.

Forget trying to defend yourself all the time. It is wiser to keep on with the task at hand and trust God to vindicate you in due course. Justice will be served in His time. Don't seek your own revenge.

DON'T MISS THE CHANCE TO HELP OTHERS

Here's a fourth and final way we need to respond to unjust suffering. By God's grace, we can turn it into an opportunity to help others.

We read in Genesis 40:6–7 that Joseph took that opportunity when he saw that Pharaoh's two officials were dejected.

Joseph could have said to himself, *Look, I've got my own problems. I'm the one who should be dejected. Forget these guys.*

But the reason Joseph noticed these men were downcast is because he was looking. His head wasn't drooped so low by his own grief that he couldn't see the needs of others.

I once read about a seminary professor who went into a depression so deep that he didn't care about anyone or anything. Everything seemed hopeless.

One day a visiting friend urged him to think of people who had been of major help to him, and from that list to select one person to whom to write a letter expressing his gratitude.

The man thought about it for some time, and into his mind's eye came the face of a schoolteacher he had had when he was a small boy. This teacher had instilled in him a love of literature, and he was grateful. So he decided to write her a letter telling her how she had inspired him.

He received a reply in the shaky handwriting of the elderly woman. The note said, "Dear William, when I read your letter I was blinded with tears, for I remember you as a little fellow in my class. You have warmed my old heart. I taught school for fifty years. Yours is the first letter of thanks I have received from a student, and I shall cherish it until I die."

With that letter, a little sliver of light came into the dungeon of this professor's life. He was encouraged to write another thank-you note to a significant person in his life, and then another and another until he had written five hundred notes of gratitude and was no longer in the depression.

Are you in a dungeon at the moment? Are circumstances closing you down that are known only to you and to God? Turn your gaze outward toward others, and you will see those who need your help.

Instead of quitting or trying to fight your way out from under unjust suffering, consider Jesus. Hang in there, and keep running the race (Hebrews 12:1–2).

Now we may be tempted to say, "If I'm going to have to

take these elbows in the ribs and kicks in the shins, I don't want to be in this race."

But then we look at Christ. And our mouths are closed. We see Jesus on the cross and hear Him say, "Father, forgive them, for they do not know what they are doing" (Luke 23:34). We consider the roll call of the faithful in Hebrews 11, of those who endured so much, and we keep on running.

Chapter   Eight

ℒESSONS FROM THE DUNGEON

"Everything that was written in the past was written to teach us, so that through endurance and the encouragement of the Scriptures we might have hope" (Romans 15:4).

As we continue to see the impact of God's hand on Joseph's life in an Egyptian dungeon we continue to learn just how it is that all things work for the good of those who love Him—and Joseph's experience does offer us "the encouragement of the Scriptures" that Paul speaks of.

You'll recall that two of Joseph's fellow prisoners were servants of Pharaoh and were in jail because they had displeased their master. Each of them, the baker and the cupbearer, had a dream (Genesis 40:5), and Joseph noticed that they were disturbed.

In the process of interpreting the men's dreams and seeing the fulfillment worked out in their lives, Joseph teaches us valuable lessons from the dungeon.

LIVING WITH A GOD-CENTERED FOCUS

Here's the first lesson, illustrated in Joseph's response to the men. The message comes to us forcibly in Genesis 40:8: "We both had dreams," the two said to Joseph, "but there is no one to interpret them."

Joseph responded, "Do not interpretations belong to God?

Tell me your dreams" (v. 8). Clearly, Joseph had a unique gift from God in the ability to correctly interpret dreams. But his perspective was clear. He didn't boast of his skill or seek to draw attention to himself. He pointed to God as the source of his gift and gave Him the glory.

Using Our God-Given Gifts

There is an obvious lesson in this for us. All of us as believers have been given spiritual gifts by the Holy Spirit (1 Corinthians 12:7–11). Some people's gifts are more evident and more abundant than the gifts of others—but since all of us are gifted by God's hand, we had better not call too much attention to ourselves. For in doing so, we may obscure the grace of God.

Joseph was an early example of this principle, which runs throughout the whole of Scripture. Jesus' classic statement of it is found in the book of John:

> "Remain in me, and I will remain in you. No branch can bear fruit by itself; it must remain in the vine. Neither can you bear fruit unless you remain in me. I am the vine; you are the branches. If a man remains in me and I in him, he will bear much fruit; apart from me you can do nothing." (John 15:4–5)

Jesus means exactly what He says. Colossians 1:17 says of Christ, "He is before all things, and in him all things hold together." None of us can even breathe without His enabling. When we begin to live in the light of this truth, we will be moving from a self-centered focus to a God-centered focus.

Dealing with Our Circumstances

The way we react to circumstances also reveals our focus. An amateur photographer doesn't always capture the image on which he thought he had trained his camera. So when he gets his pictures back, he might see a drainpipe coming out of someone's head or a building that's only half in the frame.

He might look at the bad pictures and say, "This isn't what

I was photographing." But the fact is, what shows up in the photos is exactly what was in the lens. The photos reveal the photographer's focus in an undeniable way.

In the same way, Joseph's reaction to all that happened to him revealed an incredibly God-centered life. We've said it before, but it bears repeating here. There was no self-pity and complaining recorded of this godly young man.

Turn over a page to Genesis 41:15–16, and you'll see the focus of Joseph's life making itself known again. This time Pharaoh had a dream, and the cupbearer finally remembered there was a Hebrew prisoner in the dungeon who could interpret dreams.

Pharaoh sent for Joseph and said, "I have heard it said of you that when you hear a dream you can interpret it" (v. 15). Underline Joseph's response. "I cannot do it . . . but God will give Pharaoh the answer he desires" (v. 16).

"I cannot do it." Those are four of the most important words for anybody who wants to be used by God. That is the first thing you and I need to know. *We cannot do it.* And if we think we can, we need to step aside and sit down.

The next two words Joseph spoke were even more important: "But God." I can't, *but God can.* My need of Him is total. That's what it means to have a God-centered focus.

We see this perspective on Joseph's part again in Genesis 45. By then he was in charge of Egypt, administering the food during the great famine. His brothers stood in front of him, at his mercy.

As Joseph explained to them what had happened to him, he said, "*But God* sent me ahead of you to preserve for you a remnant on earth and to save your lives" (v. 7, italics added). Then verse 8 tells us that he said again, "It was not you who sent me here, *but God*" (italics added).

There are those two words again. Joseph could say this about the years of mistreatment and suffering that had befallen him because his focus was on the right person.

Seeing the Big Picture

Joseph was learning to live a God-focused life in the dungeon. Even in the darkness, he was able to see his life from a perspective bigger than his immediate surroundings.

Do you want to live with a self-centered focus? Be prepared for major disappointment. Do you want to live with a circumstance-centered focus? Be prepared for endless frustration. The only way to live is joyfully with a God-centered focus. That's when you will be looking in the right direction.

Occasionally I have conversations with people who are still looking for themselves. I understand why they haven't found themselves yet. They're looking in the wrong direction. They don't have a God-centered focus. I have to tell them, "You're not going to find yourself until you meet God."

People don't know how to view themselves because our culture, and particularly the university establishment, has fed them a confusing array of false worldviews.

The result is that many people are like the guy who jumped off the top of a thirty-five-story building. As he passed the twentieth floor, somebody heard him shout, "So far, so good."

That's the way many people are living. They're just hanging on from weekend to weekend. The only answer to this kind of emptiness and hopelessness is the answer provided in this lesson from the dungeon.

John Calvin figured this out more than four hundred years ago. "Man never achieves a clear knowledge of himself. He can never know who he is unless he has first looked upon God's face and then descends from contemplating Him to scrutinizing himself."

Without a God-centered focus to life, everything is turned on its head. You will never know who you are, why you are here, or what you are supposed to be doing until first you gaze into the face of God as revealed in the person of the Lord Jesus Christ. When you acknowledge Christ for who He is, then you will discover who you are.

TELLING THE TRUTH

A second lesson from the dungeon is the importance of telling the truth without ambiguity, whether it's good news or bad news.

As soon as Pharaoh's cupbearer told Joseph his dream, Joseph came back with the interpretation (Genesis 40:12–13). By telling the man that the three branches he saw were three days, after which he would be restored to his position, Joseph was putting his truthfulness on the line. It would have been the height of foolishness for him to make such a prediction without the authority of God behind him. But that's what Joseph had.

He also told the truth to Pharaoh's baker without stuttering when the baker came to Joseph hoping for the same good news the cupbearer had heard (v. 16).

The baker had seen the change in the cupbearer's countenance and had come to Joseph. "Hey, that was a nice thing you said to the cupbearer. I liked that. Three days and then back on the job. Well, I had a dream as well. Let me tell you what I dreamed, so you can give me a good interpretation too." But Joseph's interpretation was a prediction of the baker's death (vv. 18–19).

Maybe the baker thought that since he and the other man were in the same circumstances, he could expect the same outcome as his neighbor.

But here's a lesson within a lesson. George Lawson points out, "Let us remember that divine providence is under no obligation to be equally kind to us all. And that prosperity and adversity, life and death, are distributed to men by One who has a right to do what He will with His own." In other words, God is God, and He can do what He likes.

Now it would have been easy for Joseph to soothe this man and tell him some sweet little lies. After all, in three days he would be dead, so there would be nothing to answer for in Joseph's case if he lied to him.

There are plenty of people in the pulpits of our churches

who are willing to soothe the feelings of spiritually dying men and women, to assure them they are all right. But when you're dealing with matters of eternity, do you really want to go someplace where someone will tell you lies?

The lesson from the dungeon is that if you are going to be the servant of God, you're going to have to tell the truth—the good, the bad, and the ugly—no matter what. And you're going to have to live with the blast furnace of criticism and opposition.

Witness the integrity of Joseph in this matter. Some people must have looked at him years later and said, "He became the prime minister of Egypt overnight."

No, he didn't. God was fashioning Joseph for leadership in the crucible of suffering, hammering out his convictions on the anvil of life. And one thing God was teaching Joseph was this: "Joseph, tell the truth. Do what is right, because it is always right to do right." Joseph learned the lesson, and he stood out in the midst of the malaise around him.

Just before his death, Paul told his spiritual son and disciple, Timothy, "Preach the Word. . . . For the time will come when men will not put up with sound doctrine. Instead, to suit their own desires, they will gather around them a great number of teachers to say what their itching ears want to hear" (2 Timothy 4:2–3). Calvin says, "All love to be flattered. Hence the majority of teachers, in desiring to yield to the corrupt wishes of the world, adulterate the Word of God."

Joseph told the truth in the dungeon even when it was hard. What a shame that our nation is led for the most part not by people of this commitment, but by politicians who wait to see what popular sentiment is at the moment, and then follow it.

Somebody has to stand up and tell the truth. If God's people will not be strong and do exploits, then who shall?

PREPARING FOR DEATH

Joseph's words to this baker must have really stung him.

Imagine knowing you have three days to live. If the baker had known what his dream was going to mean, we can presume he wouldn't have asked for the interpretation. He would rather have lived those three days in ignorance.

Lawson says of Pharaoh's baker that he died three days before his time. Thoughts of the fatal moment and of the birds feeding on his carcass must have taken possession of his soul, whether he was sleeping or awake.

The Certainty of Death and Judgment

Joseph told the baker the hard truth. You say, "Well, fortunately, we don't have to say that to anybody today." That's right; we aren't given specific prophecies of people's death to deliver to them.

But we do have an important message to deliver about death and what follows it. "Man is destined to die once, and after that to face judgment" (Hebrews 9:27). We need to say that Jesus taught more about hell than He ever taught about heaven.

We need to help people understand that they cannot have a heaven without a hell, that it is intellectually implausible to have the one without the other, and that they must prepare for the day when they will stand before God and face eternal judgment.

Do you suppose Pharaoh's baker used his final three days of his life to make preparation for his death? Perhaps he seized the chance to go back to Joseph and say, "Joseph, I'm scared to death. I don't know what it is about you, but you seem to know the true God."

Did he say, "Joseph, can you help me deal with this?" Or did he while away his final three days, doing nothing about his soul? We don't know, but we can say this: If the baker failed to make use of the time that was given him, it was his own fault.

My mother died suddenly during the routine of a very normal evening, in a very normal house, with a very normal family, as a very normal forty-seven-year-old woman. In the goodness of God she was prepared for that unanticipated moment.

Are you prepared to die? If you don't know the answer to that question, put this book down now and settle the issue with God. Don't miss this lesson from the dungeon. Pharaoh's baker and people on death row aren't the only people living with a death sentence. Death is an appointment we all must keep.

Let me tell you, the baker got a deal. He had seventy-two hours to prepare. We have no such guarantee. That is why the Bible says, "Now is the time of God's favor, now is the day of salvation" (2 Corinthians 6:2).

When it comes to preparing for death, I think of the two thieves crucified with Jesus.

Both were in immediate proximity to Christ. Both were aware of the injustice being done to Him. Both were aware of the justice being meted out to them. Both knew they were not going to leave those crosses alive.

And yet one thief cursed Jesus while the other shouted over at the first one, "Don't you fear God?" (Luke 23:40). Then he said to Jesus, "Remember me when you come into your kingdom" (v. 42). Jesus gave him the great promise, "Today you will be with me in paradise" (v. 43). I call that making preparation for death.

A Theology of Death and Dying

One of the great challenges we face at the turn of the millennium is to learn how to cope with the fact that we are living longer and that the process of death has become for many far more protracted than it was in an earlier time.

We have to develop an approach to terminal care that allows the individual who is facing death to balance hope with reality. In hoping and praying for continuances of life we must learn to prepare for death. If we are not prepared for this "final journey," then we are building castles in the air, constructing houses on sand instead of on the solid rock of Jesus' words regarding resurrection and life.

"To tell or not to tell," that is the question when someone

in the family is gravely ill. Should we confront our family member with abrupt and unguarded revelations about the imminence of his demise?

Every circumstance will need to be considered on its own merits, but probably not. We will be the most help to the one facing a grave illness when we remind him of the uncertainty of his condition and and allow him to face the possibility—or even the probability—that he will not recover.

When I sat at my father's hospital bedside a few days before he passed away, I was in no doubt that he was aware of his circumstances.

In dealing with death as a pastor over the years I observed that circumstances like my father's are common. The human frame is increasingly alert to its demise. We do best by helping one another to face the prospect gradually rather than waiting until the pain medication takes the sufferer into a state that makes communication impossible.

Let us beware of sharing platitudes with the dying that may ease our discomfort but do little for them. Honesty with wisdom and grace is always the best policy. The assistance we should provide is not that which shocks them into an untimely passing but that which enables them to rest in the promises of God's Word.

And what of you?

Do you have a theology that prepares you for death? Let me suggest one. Any view of life and death that does not come to grips with John 11:25 is deficient. Jesus told His friend Martha, "I am the resurrection and the life. He who believes in me will live, even though he dies; and whoever lives and believes in me will never die."

We cannot really begin to live until we have faced with composure the reality of death and have prepared for it by faith in Jesus Christ. Are you prepared to die? If so, you are prepared to live. We don't know what happened to Pharaoh's baker. Don't let that same question mark hang over your life.

DEALING WITH DISAPPOINTMENT

A fourth lesson from the dungeon concerns dealing with disappointment and unfulfilled hopes.

Have you ever been disappointed by events or people? Ever had desires and dreams and hopes that went unfulfilled? We've all had them. They are part of the package called life.

From the human standpoint, Joseph's life up to this point could be viewed as a series of crushing disappointments and shattered dreams. And in the dungeon in Egypt, he was about to suffer yet another setback: "The chief cupbearer, however, did not remember Joseph; he forgot him" (Genesis 40:23).

I imagine that on the day of his release, the man grabbed Joseph by the hand and said, "Joseph, thanks for what you did for me. You can expect to hear from me. I'm your man, Joe."

Have you ever heard those words from somebody, and six months later your phone still hasn't rung? Perhaps someone you thought loved you told you, "I'm yours," and then left, never to be heard from again.

How do we deal with the disappointment of unfulfilled dreams? How do we deal with the fact that people just flat out let us down sometimes? Let's learn something important from Joseph.

We can only assume that there was a great expectation in Joseph's heart as the cupbearer was restored to his position. In those first days after the cupbearer's release, Joseph's spirit probably quickened every time he heard a rattling at the door of the dungeon. "They're coming to release me."

Putting it in contemporary terms, Joseph would have been saying, "If the phone rings, don't touch it. It'll be for me."

But the first call wasn't for Joseph. Neither was the second or the third. And as the days lengthened into weeks and then months, Joseph came to realize there was not going to be a call from the cupbearer.

We know from Genesis 41:1 that "two full years" passed before anyone came for Joseph. What a disappointment! But disappointments happen all the time. It's an axiom of life that people fail us and let us down. Things we hope will happen and expect to happen don't go as we anticipate. Even the best of persons will prove to be a disappointment to us at times.

Why should we be surprised? After all, we in turn fail and disappoint others. We leave projects incomplete and promises unfulfilled. This brings home graphically the words of Jeremiah 17:5: "Cursed is the one who trusts in man, who depends on flesh for his strength, and whose heart turns away from the Lord."

If you're relying on other people for your hopes and plans, your trust is in the wrong place—even more so if your confidence in yourself or others causes you to cease trusting in the Lord!

People can be secondary causes of God's provision for us, but our ultimate confidence must be in Him. Anything less than this will lead us to great disappointment and pain.

> Some will love thee,
> Some will hate thee,
> Some will praise thee,
> Some will slight.
>
> Cease from man
> And look above thee,
> Trust in God
> And do the right.

How did Joseph handle the bitter disappointment of the cupbearer's faulty memory? Judging by Joseph's conduct two years later, he kept his confidence anchored in God. If anyone had learned that people often disappoint, it was our man in Egypt!

LEARNING TO REST IN GOD'S FAITHFULNESS

Here is a fifth and final lesson we discover in the dungeon.

It's the flip side of learning to deal with disappointment. The two added years of imprisonment gave Joseph yet another chance to learn the lesson that God is faithful and that he could rest his hopes in the Lord.

How many times we must relearn the lesson that God is the only unfailing One. He is the only One who is true to His Word on every occasion. "Some trust in chariots and some in horses, but we trust in the name of the Lord our God" (Psalm 20:7).

It appeared to Joseph that he had been forgotten—and he had, by the cupbearer. But he had not been forgotten by his Lord and Master.

What do you do when you are forgotten by people? What do you do when you have taken a few too many blows to the shins, too many elbows in the ribs as you've run the race of life? Where do you turn when you are so weary you feel you cannot run another step?

What you do is look away from people and look up. When I am weary and disappointed, I go back to my Bible, where I read:

> *The Lord is the everlasting God, the Creator of the ends of the earth. He will not grow tired or weary, and his understanding no one can fathom. He gives strength to the weary and increases the power of the weak. Even youths grow tired and weary, and young men stumble and fall; but those who hope in the Lord will renew their strength. They will soar on wings like eagles; they will run and not grow weary, they will walk and not be faint.* (Isaiah 40:28–31)

What tremendous promises to the weak and weary. That's all of us at one time or another. If you can learn to rest in God's faithfulness, you can sleep secure in any storm.

One evening I was on an airline flight, seated next to a young family. The smaller of the two children was seated between her mother and me. We were at the rear of the plane, where the roar of the engines was very pronounced.

In the course of that flight, the mother gathered her wee one into her lap and nestled her under her chin. And the little girl fell sound asleep with her face mashed up against her mother's breast.

What a wonderful picture of resting in God's care. This wee one was traveling at six hundred miles per hour in a steel tube thirty-five thousand feet above the ground, and yet she didn't have a care in the world. She was with her mom, and she knew her mom would hold her fast.

Wouldn't it be great to be loved like that? To be loved the way a mother loves her precious child? If I could write songs, I'd write a song about that, because that's the way God loves you and me.

Listen to God's word to his people through Isaiah: "Can a mother forget the baby at her breast and have no compassion on the child she has borne? Though she may forget, I will not forget you! See, I have engraved you on the palms of my hands" (Isaiah 49:15–16).

The hand of God under which His servant Joseph lived was engraved with the young man's name. So let us learn to rest upon Him, and even the dungeon can become for us a place of peace and comfort.

$\mathcal{P}$HARAOH'S DREAM AND JOSEPH'S PLAN

It's amazing what can happen in the small space between two chapters in our Bible.

As quickly as the Pentateuch writer, Moses, recorded that Joseph was forgotten by Pharaoh's cupbearer after the latter's release from prison (Genesis 40:23), the text jumps ahead two years to the events recorded in 41:1.

Now whether these two years refer to the entire time Joseph was in prison or to the time following the cupbearer's release, we don't know for sure. But either way, the point is that Joseph was in the dungeon a lot longer than he would have ever imagined. He was there far too long for someone who had done nothing to deserve imprisonment.

The good fortune of Pharaoh's close servant in being let out of prison gave Joseph a little glimmer of hope for his own release. But as we saw in the previous chapter, that glimmer dimmed and died as the months went by with no word.

During that time Joseph might have prayed with the psalmist, "How long, O Lord? Will you forget me forever? How long will you hide your face from me?" (Psalm 13:1).

THE PATIENCE OF JOSEPH

There is a lesson for us in Joseph's long wait. We need to learn the patience he displayed. We have said that Joseph was a life-sized illustration of Romans 8:28, the fact that "in all things God works for the good of those who love him, who have been called according to his purpose."

We need to understand that although our days may seem dark, and although there seems to be no potential for change, nevertheless God is working everything out in conformity with the purpose of His will. And He makes everything beautiful in His time (Ecclesiastes 3:11).

That's what Joseph was about to discover when the word finally came, "Get up, shave yourself, and get dressed. Pharaoh has sent for you." Joseph got to see the end of God's purpose in his life, and he could say it was good.

But not all of God's heroes got to see the fulfillment of His promises and His work in their lives. The writer of Hebrews says, "These people were still living by faith when they died. They did not receive the things promised; they only saw them and welcomed them from a distance. And they admitted that they were aliens and strangers on earth" (Hebrews 11:13).

It takes patience to live a life like that. It takes patience to be faithful under those conditions, when you are not seeing the promised fulfillment and you're not always sure what God is doing in your life.

Two years passed with no good word for Joseph. Reading this, I need to be reminded that God knows what is best for each of His children. We do well to wait upon Him, for He will never give us anything too soon, nor will anything ever arrive too late.

But we want to ask, when will the promise arrive? When will the answer come? We want to believe God, but we're not so sure we can hang in there if it's not going to happen soon.

We often hear people complain that their lives are monotonous. Well, in one sense life *is* monotonous. Most of us do basically the same things every day. We get up, get dressed, have breakfast, and drive the same route to the same workplace. We drive the same route back to the same house, and the next day repeat the same routine. There is a lack of variety, but—and this is vitally important—God is sovereign in these kinds of days. It is in the routines of life that real gains are made, real joy is found, and the reality of God's provision becomes most obvious.

So many books on marriage highlight the need for dramatic interludes. While it is beneficial to enjoy such changes, to think that a week on the beach in Hawaii is going to fix everything is to be sadly misled. God works patience into us in the routine of our days.

So it is that in the midst of the humdrum we learn patience. It surely doesn't get more monotonous than being chained to a dungeon wall for two years, but Joseph waited on God—and God sovereignly stirred the mind of Pharaoh.

THE TROUBLED MIND OF PHARAOH

Pharaoh had two dreams that deeply troubled him. In the first dream, seven sleek cows were eaten by seven ugly cows (Genesis 41:2–4). In the second dream, seven full heads of grain were consumed by seven thin heads of grain (vv. 5–7).

The result of Pharaoh's dreams was that "in the morning his mind was troubled" (v. 8). He awakened with a sense of foreboding. So, like Humpty-Dumpty, who fell off the wall, he called for all the king's horses and all the king's men to put things together.

Pharaoh's circumstances and dreams were unique to him, but we, too, know what it is to awaken cold and troubled. Sometimes we have tried to warm ourselves by the blanket of materialism or self-sufficiency—but had to admit that the covering is insufficient. Such an experience may have proven to be for us, as it was for Pharaoh, a moment of opportunity. When our circumstances are happy and prosperous, we have little sense of our need to hear from one of God's servants. When we awaken in a cold sweat, we will be glad to find someone like Joseph nearby.

But no one could interpret the king's dreams. Presumably, all Pharaoh's wise men could do was look down at the floor in embarrassment. "We're sorry, but you've stumped us on this one."

Now in those days if royal astrologers or wise men failed to interpret a king's dreams, it could cost them their heads. King Nebuchadnezzar ordered all the wise men of Babylon put to death when they could not interpret his dream (Daniel 2:1–13). Daniel saved the day in that case.

So we can assume the Egyptian court officials were in trouble. But suddenly the cupbearer shook the cobwebs off of his memory and said, "Your Highness, I just remembered that a young Hebrew who was in prison with me and the chief baker interpreted our dreams for us, and everything turned out exactly as he said" (see Genesis 41:9–13).

"So Pharaoh sent for Joseph" (v. 14). The king was so disturbed that he was ready to hear from a forgotten prisoner in the royal dungeon. Joseph hurriedly cleaned up, put on some fresh clothes, and was hustled into the king's presence. It was quite a conversation:

"Pharaoh said to Joseph, 'I had a dream, and no one can interpret it. But I have heard it said of you that when you hear a dream you can interpret it.'

"'I cannot do it,' Joseph replied to Pharaoh, "but God will give Pharaoh the answer he desires'" (vv. 15–16).

In Joseph's simple, straightforward answer to Pharaoh is the nature of all genuine Christian service and, indeed, the nature of all spiritual life.

We do not find coming from the lips of Joseph any proud assertions about what he is going to do and how he is going to do it. He lived in the awareness that God is sovereign, that it is He who orders our steps and marks them out before us.

THE INTERPRETATION GOD PROVIDED

It is remarkable how many of the commentaries on this portion of Scripture refer to the interpretation of Pharaoh's dreams as Joseph's interpretation. But Joseph made clear to Pharaoh that he couldn't give an interpretation in his own wisdom (v. 16). Only God was able to do such things.

The Importance of a God-Focused Life

We pointed to this verse in the previous chapter as evidence that Joseph's entire existence was God-focused, not self-focused. We will see this same quality in Genesis 41:51–52, when we read that Joseph named his two sons Manasseh and Ephraim.

The boys' names mean, respectively, "one who causes to forget," and "fruitful," because Joseph was acknowledging that God had caused him to forget his sufferings and had made him fruitful in Egypt. In other words, you could not even meet Joseph's family without being reminded how keenly aware Joseph was of God's providential dealings with him. The imprint of God's hand was everywhere in Joseph's life.

So it is no surprise that in the matter of Pharaoh's dream, *God* was the first word on Joseph's lips. In verse 25, he said to Pharaoh, "God has revealed to Pharaoh what he is about to do." Again, in verse 32, "The matter has been firmly decided by God, and God will do it soon."

These verses express Joseph's core conviction about the fact of God's providence. He recognized that God determines what is going to happen according to His will, for His glory, and for the good of His people. All the way through the account of Joseph's life, this remarkable man acknowledged that God was the speaker of His Word and the doer of His works.

This is crucial to reaffirm in a world where, for the past thirty years, God has been downsized and people exalted. Joseph's perspective was unmistakable, and he was not alone in emphasizing God's sovereign hand.

We read in Isaiah 45:5, "I am the Lord, and there is no other; apart from me there is no God." We read of wisdom in Proverbs 8:15–16: "By me [wisdom] kings reign; . . . by me princes govern." Why would unbelieving men and women seek to deny the declaration of the God who rules all? After all, written into their very being is an awareness of God and a sense of eternity. They have at least the sneaking suspicion that Isaiah 45:5 is true. "I am the Lord, and there is no other."

The problem is people's refusal to acknowledge the God who made them, and thus their denial of His sovereign rule. "For although they knew God, they neither glorified Him as God nor gave thanks to Him, but their thinking became futile and their foolish hearts were darkened" (Romans 1:21). Joseph was a wonder because he recognized God's sovereign, overruling power. Look also at Isaiah 45: "It is I who made the earth and created mankind upon it. My own hands stretched out the heavens; I marshaled their starry hosts" (v. 12).

"I'm in charge!" That's what God is saying. He was in charge of Joseph's circumstances and of Pharaoh's dreams, and He is in charge today. This is so contrary to the prevailing worldview. It is diametrically opposed to the thinking we live with day in, day out.

But the challenge is always this: Are men and women going to allow the Word of God to sit in judgment on their puny minds, or are they going to make their puny minds the judges of the Word of God?

We have taken the latter course as a culture. So there is mass confusion today—even in the evangelical church—over whether the Bible is true and over how far we should go in obeying it.

What a sad contrast to the life of Joseph. He had slept in the dungeon but would soon be sleeping in Pharaoh's palace, because he believed in the providence of God. What an encouragement to us to know that whether we are in chains or in the king's chariot, God is working all things out for His glory and our good. It is that Biblical doctrine that will enable us to keep on an even keel in the storms of life.

The Urgency of the Situation

So Joseph told Pharaoh that Egypt would experience seven years of abundance followed by seven years of famine. The famine would be so severe that the good years preceding it would be forgotten (Genesis 41:30–31).

Then Joseph explained that the reason God gave Pharaoh the dream in two forms was that God had firmly decided what He was going to do (v. 32). This was a matter of grave urgency.

THE PLAN JOSEPH SUGGESTED

Joseph had more than an accurate interpretation of Pharaoh's dream. He had a plan.

Joseph's Wise Proposal

We don't know whether Pharaoh would have benefited from Joseph's interpretation without Joseph's follow-up proposal. Joseph sensed the importance of applying the revelation he had received, so his suggested plan was clear and straightforward:

> *"Now let Pharaoh look for a discerning and wise man and put him in charge of the land of Egypt. Let Pharaoh appoint commissioners over the land to take a fifth of the harvest of Egypt during the seven years of abundance. They should collect all the food of these good years that are coming and store up the grain under the authority of Pharaoh, to be kept in the cities for food. This food should be held in reserve for the country, to be used during the seven years of famine that will come upon Egypt, so that the country may not be ruined by the famine." (vv. 33–36)*

Someone has said the world will always make way for the person who knows where he is going—and Joseph knew where he was going.

Why was it so important that a "discerning and wise" person be chosen to administer Egypt's famine relief plan? Because the circumstances were so grave and so much was at stake. And because such a powerful position could tempt the person in it to graft, bribery, and all kinds of corruption. So what was needed was a wise and honest person, not just a personality. What a word of needed rebuke to the spirit of our age. We don't have heroes to offer, just celebrities—people who stare at us from the pages of the magazines at the grocery store.

Who are these people? What did they ever do? What makes them famous? They didn't win a Nobel Prize. They didn't write a great book. They didn't give their lives in the cause of society. They're just famous for being famous—and in some cases, for being infamous. They're famous only because this is the era of personality, not of character.

Joseph also told Pharaoh that when he found this famine-relief administrator, he needed to put him in charge of Egypt.

Now wait a minute. Joseph was speaking to the person who was already in charge of Egypt. Twenty-four hours before, this Hebrew slave had been languishing in prison. Now he was telling the king, "This is what you need to do."

Why didn't Pharaoh command Joseph to be dragged out and beheaded? Because the king recognized the wisdom in what this young Hebrew was saying. And why not? Joseph's suggestion that Egypt store up 20 percent of the food produced in the good years was a smart plan.

In fact, Joseph had done the math in such a way that Egypt would not only have enough food for its own people during the famine, but would also have a surplus to sell to surrounding countries.

Joseph's Smart Goals

Pharaoh couldn't argue with Joseph's goal, either: "So that the country may not be ruined by the famine" (Genesis 41:36).

We have said that Joseph's goals for Egypt's survival were *smart*. Someone has made this word into an acrostic for goal setting that may be helpful for you in your planning. Here is what S-M-A-R-T goals entail.

First, smart goals are *specific*. Joseph told Pharaoh in detail what needed to happen, specifying the people and the system necessary to store up the food.

Second, smart goals are *measurable*. Joseph suggested a 20 percent collection for the surplus, an easily measurable amount.

A third characteristic of smart goals is that they are *action-oriented*. Joseph's plan would have everybody in Egypt moving into action to implement it. Even Pharaoh had to get moving by finding an able administrator to oversee the project.

Fourth, smart goals are *realistic*. Joseph knew his plan was workable. It wasn't a pie-in-the-sky concoction, a silly idea.

Fifth, and finally, smart plans include a definite *time frame*. The time frame here was obvious, the seven years of bounty and surplus that Egypt was about to enjoy.

Joseph's Principled Plan

Joseph's plan was not only shrewd but also based solidly on principle. That doesn't surprise us, does it?

The plan Joseph suggested was based on the principle that, as the king, Pharaoh had a responsibility to use his power for the welfare of his people. In other words, we can safely say that Joseph believed in one aspect of the welfare state.

He was telling Pharaoh that with severe famine ahead, if they left it up to each Egyptian to lay aside 20 percent of his grain for the future, there weren't many people who would do it. I think Joseph knew that if the government let things drift in a laissez-faire market approach, the wealthy and powerful would arrange things so that they were taken care of while the powerless and the poor would go hungry.

Talking about welfare may make you a little edgy. But I would remind you that because of sin, there is no political system on Earth that is uniquely Christian. There is no system contrived by man of which we can say, "This is the biblical system." Those of us in the comfortable classes would do well to spend some time among those who would love to "pull themselves up by their bootstraps," but cannot.

But there was balance in Joseph's plan. "When the famine had spread over the whole country, Joseph opened the storehouses and sold grain to the Egyptians" (Genesis 41:56).

Here is a wonderful combination of welfare for those unable to provide for themselves, and yet responsibility for those who were able to pay. If any Egyptian thought he was simply going to come to the storehouse and get a free government handout without doing anything, he was mistaken.

Now if you find yourself applauding Joseph for the wisdom of his plan, I'm with you. But let me ask you a question. Are you preparing for days of spiritual famine that may lie ahead? If people will make all sorts of effort to make provision for a famine of food, should we not make provision for our spiritual welfare? Moses prayed, "Teach us to number our days aright, that we may gain a heart of wisdom" (Psalm 90:12).

Usually, the younger you are, the more time you think you have to prepare for eternity. But I'm told the average life span is some 36.8 million minutes. Of these, you will sleep away 12.3 million minutes and eat your way through another 3 million minutes. You will work for 13 million minutes, leaving you with some 8.5 million minutes to use.

But necessary daily routines, such as bathing and getting dressed, will take 1.5 million minutes of that leftover time. And if you're at least eighteen years old, you've already used a quarter of your allocated years. So in terms of undesignated time, you really have probably only 5 million minutes. That doesn't sound like a lot to me. Are you preparing for eternity?

I often challenge the young people in my church to memorize the Word of God, to get a New Testament and carry it with them wherever they go.

When I was a teenager I kept my New Testament with me. I don't say that to credit myself, or to suggest that I was a model teenager. But somehow, God in His providence brought me through all of that chaos, and I discovered that the things that seemed inconsequential at the time were in reality the most important.

There is a spiritual famine in our land. You can't go just anywhere and be fed on the milk and meat of God's Word. If you are in a church where the Bible is taught, be thankful. If not, I urge you to find such a place, for severe days of famine are coming. You and I need to use the days of our strength now to prepare for the days when strength is gone and we are facing the end of life.

Joseph was wise to prepare for seven years of physical famine. Let us learn from his wisdom to get ready spiritually for whatever the days ahead will bring. We cannot assume things will always be as they are today.

THE ROLE PHARAOH CREATED

By the time of the events recorded at the end of Genesis 41, there is no doubt that Joseph was in charge of things in Egypt. He was thirty years old (v. 46), so he had been in Egypt for thirteen years (cf. Genesis 37:2). After Joseph interpreted Pharaoh's dream, the king told him, "I hereby put you in charge of the whole land of Egypt" (41:41). He made Joseph his "second-in-command" (v. 43) and gave him a new name and a wife (v. 45).

Pharaoh turned the whole operation over to him. Joseph was the focus of attention. For the next seven years he went throughout Egypt making preparations for the famine. And when the famine hit with severity (v. 55) and the people cried to Pharaoh for food, Pharaoh told them, "Go to Joseph and do what he tells you."

Does that sound familiar to you? It should. As we have pointed out along the way, Joseph foreshadows the One to whom we go when faced with the great spiritual famine in our lives. At the wedding in Cana of Galilee, Jesus' mother, Mary, told the servants concerning Him, "Do whatever he tells you" (John 2:5). And the miraculous provision of wine followed.

Going to Joseph was the answer to the famine in Egypt. Going to Jesus was the answer to the lack of wine at the wedding. And going to Jesus is the answer to the spiritual famine that sin brings upon us.

Jesus says, "I am the bread life. He who comes to me will never go hungry" (John 6:35). He cried out at the great feast of unleavened bread, "If anyone is thirsty, let him come to me and drink" (John 7:37).

You may say, "You know, Alistair, I'm seriously considering giving my life to Jesus, and I think I will someday." If you are delaying that decision, let me remind you what happened to others who waited before preparing for spiritual famine. The story is in the parable of the ten virgins in Matthew 25:1–13.

You'll read that the five foolish virgins did not make adequate preparation for the bridegroom's coming, a picture of Jesus' return. As a result, when He came at an unexpected hour, they were out of oil and were barred from the wedding feast. I cannot press the urgency of this on you too strongly. Joseph knew he had seven long years to prepare for famine, yet he began right away. We are not even guaranteed tomorrow. Should we not prepare today?

Joseph is an actual historical figure who executed a real plan to deal with a real famine in Egypt. But don't read his story without seeing in it also the finger of God pointing forward to Jesus and His supply for our spiritual famine. Through this account Jesus is saying to men and women, "Come to Me with your famine. Come to Me with your emptiness. Come to Me, and you will never hunger or thirst again."

ᴊHREE CRUCIAL CONVERSATIONS

ıı "The Lord foils the plans of the nations; he thwarts the
purposes of the peoples. But the plans of the Lord
stand firm forever, the purposes of his heart through all generations" (Psalm 33:10–11).

The absence of food is not a passing matter. It means life or
death. The scenes of drought and starvation from the heartland
of Africa with which we have grown sadly too familiar will help
us imagine the situation in which we find Joseph's family.

JACOB'S INSTRUCTIONS TO HIS SONS

The opening words of Genesis 42 shift the scene from Egypt
to Canaan. Twenty long years have passed since we have heard
anything from the family of Jacob. But even though the years
have been silent, God has been at work in incredible ways in
Egypt. The family's salvation from the terrible famine was already in place in the person of the second-in-command, Joseph.
The purpose for which God had permitted all of Joseph's trials
was ready to be revealed: "the saving of many lives" (50:20).

A Question

We know Jacob had many people to provide for, because
later on at least seventy people moved to Egypt when Joseph
brought his family to be with him. So when Jacob heard there

was food in Egypt, he said to his sons, "Why do you just keep looking at each other?" (Genesis 42:1).

Now this is a classic parental question. It's the kind of question children don't understand until they in turn become parents and find themselves asking the same thing. Mothers often start asking their children this question two or three days into summer vacation from school. The kids are sitting around bored, staring at each other, when Mom says, "Why are you just sitting here looking at each other?" In other words, "Why don't you go out and find something to do?"

We can imagine the situation in Jacob's family. Aimless, these grown men were sitting around, looking about the tent at one another, each one realizing the gravity of their need and yet each one hoping the other would come up with an idea to keep them from starving. But nobody said a word. They displayed by their posture a striking lack of initiative!

A Word of Direction

So Jacob followed up his question with a word of direction. "I have heard that there is grain in Egypt. Go down there and buy some for us, so that we may live and not die" (v. 2).

Jacob was clearly a man who trusted in God. But trust in God is always accompanied by action. Jacob's trust that God would provide did not cause him to sit around and wait for God to drop food from the sky. Jacob took the initiative, asking and seeking and knocking (see Matthew 7:7–11). God's blessings are not the portion of the lazy. The psalmist says, "Trust in the Lord and do good" (Psalm 37:3).

A Step of Protection

Jacob sent his sons to Egypt—but not all of them. Only the guilty ten were dispatched.

"Jacob did not send Benjamin, Joseph's brother, with the others, because he was afraid that harm might come to him" (Genesis 42:4). We already know why Jacob clung so tightly to his youngest son. Benjamin was not only the baby but also, like Joseph, was the son of Jacob's beloved Rachel.

Jacob had already gone through the dreadful experience of saying good-bye to Joseph, believing he was going away for only a few days, and yet failing to see him return. Jacob was determined he was not going to risk that pain again. He was willing for the older sons to go, but not Benjamin.

JOSEPH'S CONVERSATION WITH HIS BROTHERS

The second conversation in this passage begins in verse 7b, but the context is set for us in verses 5–7a, which tell us that Joseph's ten brothers made their way to Egypt and became part of the long line of people waiting to purchase grain from Joseph.

The Brothers Appear in Egypt

The brothers came before the governor of Egypt and bowed down, thus fulfilling Joseph's dream concerning them (Genesis 37:7). They did not know the governor was Joseph, of course, but he recognized them.

Picture the scene with me for a moment. Here was a group of dusty, tired, middle-aged Hebrew shepherds and farmers coming into the dazzling court of Egypt. Their beards had grayed, their hair had fallen out a little, and they had been weathered by the sun and buffeted by life. They had wives and children at home, and they had come in obedience to their father's direction.

These men were just part of a throng of hungry people, a succession of folks coming to Egypt because Egypt had become the soup kitchen of the world. We can imagine the emotions that must have stirred in Joseph's heart as he looked out over this sea of gaunt faces, people facing the prospect of famine and death, and spotted his brothers.

The Approach of Joseph

Before making himself known to them, Joseph wanted to

find out something. So, the text says, "as soon as Joseph saw his brothers, he recognized them, but he pretended to be a stranger and spoke harshly to them. 'Where do you come from?' he asked" (v. 7).

You might wonder why his brothers didn't recognize Joseph. But remember, twenty years had passed. Look at your high school yearbook photo and then look in the mirror, and see if you have changed. Even if it's only been twenty years since you graduated, chances are you don't look very much like that picture.

Besides the years that had passed, everything about Joseph had changed. After tearing off his coat, his brothers had left him in rags, and now he stood before them in the regal finery of an Egyptian governor. Even his language had changed. Joseph was speaking to them through an interpreter (v. 23).

Besides all the changes, consider this. Even if the brothers entertained any thought of looking for Joseph when they went to Egypt, where would they have looked? In the slave markets, no doubt, or the refugee camps where foreigners lived. They would have looked for someone of obvious Hebrew descent. The last place they would look would be Pharaoh's palace.

It's interesting to note that as Joseph looked at his brothers, he remembered his dreams (v. 9). And he needed to find out whether they still hated him or whether they felt any sorrow for their sin or sense of remorse or guilt over their actions. So Joseph decided to conceal his identity until he got the answers. God was using the brothers' trip to Egypt to bring them face-to-face with their long-concealed sin.

The Accusation by Joseph

Joseph accused his brothers of spying. "You are spies! You have come to see where our land is unprotected" (v. 9). They reacted to the accusation, denying it categorically (v. 10).

Now get this scene in mind. Remember, these ten brothers were rough chaps. They had laid waste to the city of Shechem all by themselves. They had murdered every male in the place in reprisal for the violation of their sister, Dinah.

These men were not used to having some finely dressed dandy they didn't even know accuse them of spying. You can almost imagine a couple of them reaching for their swords, thinking, "I'll show him spies!"

But if they were angry at all, that emotion was swallowed up by fear. For the fact was that they were in a foreign land being accused of a capital crime against that country. And so they protested their innocence by saying, "We are all the sons of one man. Your servants are honest men, not spies" (v. 11).

Why did these men mention they were brothers? It wasn't just for Joseph's information. They were saying that no sensible man who wanted to engage in spying would run the risk of losing his entire family in the operation. He might send one or two sons on the mission, or maybe three, but not all ten.

Besides, what kind of spy operation would send ten people parading around in the open? Spies operate covertly, in the dark, behind closed doors and in secret meetings. I've never seen a spy movie in which the spies went around in groups of ten.

Peeling Away the Layers

Joseph knew this, of course, but he pushed them again, repeating his charge (v. 12). And as a result, the layers of all the brothers' consciences began to peel away. "Your servants were twelve brothers, the sons of one man, who lives in the land of Canaan. The youngest is now with our father, and one is no more" (v. 13).

Of course, the brothers didn't know they were talking to "Mr. No More"! Here is the very definition of irony. When I get to heaven, I'm going to ask Joseph how he felt when his brothers said, "One is no more." Whatever his reaction, he maintained his cover and repeated his charge of spying a third time.

Why this particular charge? Spying may have been a problem during this time of worldwide famine, as desperate nations tried to find a way into Egypt to steal some of the produce. But I think it was more than that. Joseph was holding a mirror up to his brothers, reminding them of what had happened to him twenty years before.

Do you recall what three things had annoyed the brothers about Joseph? There were his special coat and his dream, but he had also brought a bad report about the men to their father (Genesis 37:2). In other words, the brothers had seen Joseph as Jacob's spy, sent to get information and then run back to Daddy with it.

So when they had seen Joseph coming over the horizon in Dothan, the men must have determined they were not going to let this annoying little dreamer snoop on them and report back to their father. In a similar incident hundreds of years later, young David was accused by his oldest brother of coming to the Israelite camp to snoop around (see 1 Samuel 17:28).

Now indeed, Jacob *had* sent Joseph with instructions to "bring word back to [him]" on the brothers (Genesis 37:14). But there was no sense in which he sent Joseph as a spy.

The problem here was in the minds of the brothers. When you're up to dirty business, when you don't have a clear conscience because you're doing things you shouldn't be doing, you're suspicious of everyone and on the defensive even in normal situations.

So Joseph decided to accuse his brothers of the very thing they had held against him. Back in Dothan, Joseph had protested his innocence but had been treated with harsh words, imprisonment in a cistern, and, finally, deportation to Egypt as a slave. Now the brothers were protesting their innocence, and Joseph responded with harsh words and imprisonment (vv. 14–17).

If they had never thought of it before, these ten sons of Jacob now knew how it felt to be clapped into prison for something they didn't do. They saw their own actions in the mirror, and it wasn't pretty.

Again, Joseph was not simply being peevish and vengeful. By taking this approach, he was making a powerful appeal to his brothers' consciences so that they would recognize and admit their sin against him. At any rate, they would have three days to think about it.

THE CONVERSATION AMONG JOSEPH'S BROTHERS

On the third day, Joseph had his brothers brought before him again. He had told them earlier that he was going to keep nine of them in prison and let one go back (v. 16). But now he decided to keep one in prison (it would be Simeon) and send the nine back (vv. 18–20, 24). Either way, however, they had to bring Benjamin with them when they returned to Egypt.

Having set down the conditions, Joseph fell silent as a conversation ensued among his brothers. They didn't bother to disguise their thoughts, since "they did not realize that Joseph could understand them" (v. 23).

A Revealing Discussion

This was a very revealing discussion, for more than ever before in their lives these men now gave an explanation of their hearts and their actions. The talk was so emotionally charged that when they finished, Joseph had to turn away from them and weep (v. 24).

"They said to one another, 'Surely we are being punished because of our brother. We saw how distressed he was when he pleaded with us for his life, but we would not listen; that's why this distress has come upon us'" (v. 21).

Reuben then added, "Didn't I tell you not to sin against the boy? But you wouldn't listen! Now we must give an accounting for his blood" (v. 22).

What an emotionally charged atmosphere this was! What painful memories were being dredged up for all eleven brothers. Isn't it interesting that the ten guessed immediately why this Egyptian official had put them in prison? God uses encounters like these to bring us back to the place of our disobedience and rebellion.

This was a painful time, but it was also a red-letter day in the lives of these fellows. For twenty years they had been living a lie, keeping up the pretense with their father, making him think that Joseph was "no more" and watching their father suffer. They had been callous in the way they treated Joseph, and two decades of deceit had no doubt hardened their hearts even more. But here the first chink began to appear in the armor of their lies.

Anyone who assumes these men never gave the incident a second thought doesn't know much about human nature. If, as we suggested earlier, Joseph woke up in Egypt in a cold sweat on more than one night from reliving his ordeal in his sleep, don't you think his brothers did the same?

Don't you imagine they awakened in the night with dreams so vivid they perspired and put their hands over their ears because they could hear Joseph's cries from the pit? They lived in the shadow of their crime, waiting for the blow of judgment to fall. They admitted as much here; this was an honest conversation.

An Admission of Guilt

Up to this point Joseph's brothers had never acknowledged their guilt. Do you recall how staggered we were by their callous reaction to his cries from the pit? They sat down to eat their midday meal, choosing to ignore his pleas for mercy. Now we discover the other side of the story: We saw him; we would not listen; we must give an account.

One of the first signs of an awakening conscience is the admission of personal guilt. Some people go to church every Sunday carrying the knowledge of the pain and chaos they have caused, knowing what they have done was wrong, yet not willing to acknowledge their guilt.

But until that admission comes, there is no future for those people. God has nothing in the way of usefulness for them. What must happen is an admission of sin such as that which the Prodigal Son made when he had spent his inheritance on good times and found himself in the pigsty during a severe famine (Luke 15:11–16).

The Bible says that finally the Prodigal Son "came to his senses" (v. 17). God shook him, and he awakened spiritually and realized, "This is not my father's fault. This is not my brother's fault. I am the one to blame for my problems."

You remember the rest of the story. The young man came home utterly broken and repentant and was forgiven and restored to his position of sonship. The person who comes to Jesus like that is guaranteed an unbelievable party.

But for the stiff-necked, self-righteous Pharisees who were listening to Jesus tell this story (see Luke 15:2), there was no hope of forgiveness and restoration without the acknowledgement of personal sin and guilt.

This is why some people think they are Christians when they're not. They are prepared to acknowledge that they have made mistakes and used bad judgment, and they are ready to stop doing this and start doing that. But they are not willing to admit that they are sinners, hopelessly ruined and lost.

But without this, there can be no conversion. What the Bible calls conversion is when a person admits, "I am absolutely guilty and deserve death for my crimes. I have no excuses, and throw myself completely on the mercy of Christ. Without Him, I am utterly lost. My life is in His hands."

Isn't it interesting that Joseph, the brother against whom these ten men had sinned, was the very one who held their lives in his hands?

In Joseph's Hands

Nowhere is the hand of God more dramatically evident than in this portion of the story. God so moved and arranged events that twenty years after the crime all of the guilty offenders were delivered to the very doorstep of the brother they had offended.

But look at Joseph's attitude. Instead of lashing out against them in murderous hatred and revenge, he filled their bags with grain and said, "Take [this] back for your starving households" (Genesis 42:19).

Let's remember that these brothers hated Joseph and had once said, "We'll make sure you do not rule over us. We'll have none of that." And when they came upon him in Egypt, they didn't recognize him. Neither did they think he could understand them.

I have pointed out earlier the ways in which Joseph foreshadowed Christ. Think of the parallels. Jesus' brothers, the Israelites, "hated him and sent a delegation after him to say, 'We don't want this man to be our king'" (Luke 19:14).

When Jesus came, His fellow Israelites did not recognize Him as Messiah and did not realize He knew every word they spoke—and even understood their thoughts.

When it comes to Christ, the veil is over our hearts as well. When we wonder why the circumstances of our lives are the way they are, we need to realize that often it is God removing the props from under our lives so that He might bring us to the point to which he brought Joseph's brothers—to an awareness of our great need and then, in turn, to the discovery of God's great provision for us in Christ.

If Jacob's cupboards had been well stocked with food, Joseph's brothers would not have cared enough to make the trip to Egypt. And thus they would not have found their brother and experienced his great provision for them.

It is only when God shows us that the cupboard of our own supposed righteousness is absolutely bare that we are ready to admit our need and come humbly to Him who is the Bread of Life.

Chapter Eleven

FROM EGYPT TO CANAAN AND BACK AGAIN

The pressure in this story is building and the pace has quickened tremendously. By the time we arrive at Genesis 45:28, Joseph will have revealed himself to his brothers and Jacob knows that his long-lost son is alive. And in all the details of this saga, we see the hand of God weaving the truth of Romans 8:28 throughout every step: "We know that in all things God works for the good of those who love him, who have been called according to his purpose."

God's sovereign arrangement of events is once again obvious in this account of intrigue and surprise that is set in both Egypt and Canaan. The events were designed to test the sincerity of Joseph's ten older brothers and save the family from the severe famine that had gripped the known world. It's hard to imagine that, as the governor of Egypt (Genesis 42:6), Joseph personally handled each of the transactions made by the multitudes who lined up to purchase grain. So it was providential that he had been present on that particular occasion and had seen the faces of his ten brothers among the crowd.

THE FIRST MEETING

Put yourself in Joseph's position and try to imagine what it would be like to suddenly find yourself face-to-face with the persons who were responsible for the turmoil and suffering you had experienced over the last twenty years of your life.

Joseph's Reaction

What would come out of your heart in that moment? Would it be twenty years of hatred from the pent-up hurt? If those feelings had been inside Joseph, clearly that would have come out.

But it's obvious that God had been working in Joseph's heart—fashioning events in such a way that Joseph recognized that all of his days were under the sovereign, providential care of a God who loved him with an everlasting love.

The time had not yet come for Joseph to disclose himself to his brothers. However, he longed to see his youngest brother, Benjamin, so he decided on a plan that would bring Benjamin back to Egypt. He would detain Simeon until the others returned with Benjamin (42:18–20, 24). But he also gave the brothers ample food to take back to their families and returned each man's silver to him (42:25).

The Brothers' Discovery

Now, before we move on, notice the brothers' trembling and distress when one of them found his silver still in his sack (42:27–28). Later they were "frightened" (42:35) when it was discovered that *each* man's silver had been returned.

This event caused the brothers to ask, "What is this that God has done to us?" Even though they knew they had done nothing to cause the silver to be back in their possession, they immediately assumed they were in deep trouble.

What we are seeing here are hearts and minds set on jagged edge by twenty years of living with unrepented sin. We saw the same response earlier when Joseph accused the men of spying. Their consciences were so agitated that the slightest hint of wrongdoing or accusation brought them right back to the point of their sin and departure from God.

This was the providential hand of God in the brothers' lives—not only to bring them to repentance, but also to accomplish God's purpose of bringing Jacob's entire family to Egypt. And from that land, hundreds of years later, He would accomplish the redemption of His people Israel out of slavery, bringing them to the Land of Promise in the unfolding of His plan.

When the nine brothers returned home, they recounted to their father Jacob all that had happened to them (42:29–34). Jacob saw the grain and the silver in their sacks, but his focus was on his sons. He was understandably upset at what appeared to be the loss of Simeon, but he was particularly distressed at the news that the governor of Egypt demanded to see Benjamin before Simeon would be released (42:36–38).

Therefore, despite Reuben's drastic vow to assure Benjamin's safety, Jacob flatly refused to allow his youngest son to travel to Egypt. He said in so many words, "If anything happened to Benjamin, it would kill me." So the family settled in and began to live off the food Joseph had sent from Egypt.

THE NEED TO RETURN TO EGYPT

It's obvious from the opening words of Genesis 43 that Jacob was not going to be able to maintain his stubborn insistence that Benjamin not go to Egypt under any conditions. We are told in verse 1, "The famine was still severe in the land."

Jacob's Order

Given that circumstance, it was inevitable that Jacob's large family would sooner or later eat all the grain the brothers had brought from Egypt. How long this took we don't know, but apparently it was long enough that Jacob forgot about the demand concerning Benjamin.

As the grain ran low, Jacob told his sons, "Go back and buy us a little more food" (43:2). We find that his obstinacy was tempered by necessity. But Judah jarred his father's memory by reminding him that they did not dare to show their faces again to the governor of Egypt unless Benjamin was with them (vv. 3–5).

A little of the old Jacob appeared (v. 6) as he blamed his sons for telling Joseph they had another brother at home. Judah tried to explain that the information had come out innocently, but Jacob seemed to want to blame someone else for his sense of disquiet.

Judah's First Offer

Judah stepped forward again, offering to ensure Benjamin's safety at the cost of bearing the blame for the rest of his life if anything happened to the boy. This was the first time Judah put himself on the spot for Benjamin. We will see him do so again later in the story.

Jacob finally agreed to let Benjamin accompany his older brothers to Egypt. Jacob prepared gifts for the governor and sent the brothers off with the wistful parting, "If I am bereaved, I am bereaved" (v. 14).

God's Hand at Work

The caravan hurried off to Egypt and the brothers presented themselves to Joseph (v. 15). The rest of Genesis 43 describes the reception they received in Joseph's house.

Obviously, Joseph's brothers did not realize what they were heading into. They thought they were going back for a series of dealings with that stern governor in Egypt in the hopes of getting the food they needed and being reunited with their brother Simeon.

Based on the statement the brothers made in Genesis 42:28, "What is this that God has done to us?" it seems evident they felt that they deserved better than what had happened to them in Egypt. The answer to their question was that God overruled the details of their lives in conformity with the purpose of His will.

He does the same with us. Even though Jacob said, "Everything is against me!" (Genesis 42:36), he could have asked "If God is for us, who can be against us?" (Romans 8:31). This is the question Paul asked after making the great declaration of Romans 8:28. The answer to the apostle's question is that nobody can be against us when God is for us. He is sovereignly in charge, and we can trust Him.

Lunch with Joseph

Joseph's heart must have leapt when he saw Benjamin (Genesis 43:16). He instructed his steward to take the brothers to his home and prepare a meal for them. Once again, the brothers reveal a guilty conscience in fearing that they were being set up for an ambush (v. 18). These fellows had been waiting for God's judgment to fall for twenty years, and they feared this was it.

But Joseph's household servant assured them things were fine and brought Simeon out to eat with them. At noon the "boss" came home for what would be a most unusual luncheon.

When Joseph came home for lunch, the brothers presented him with their gifts and "bowed down before him to the ground" (v. 26). Joseph inquired about the condition of their father, and in answering the brothers bowed low again. Joseph's dream of so many years earlier was being amply fulfilled.

We know that Joseph's heart was deeply stirred, but it was when he saw Benjamin, "his own mother's son" (v. 29), that Joseph lost his composure. He had to hurry out to his private room so he could weep and release the tremendous emotions in his heart.

When Joseph had composed himself again, he came back out, and the meal was served according to Egyptian tradition, with the Hebrew visitors eating by themselves. Benjamin received five times as much food as the other brothers, perhaps another small test by Joseph to see if his brothers would react with the same resentment they had showed toward him.

THE BROTHERS' FINAL EXAM

But the brothers' final exam, if you will, was about to come. Genesis 44 records how Joseph put his brothers to the ultimate test by having his steward plant his silver cup in Benjamin's sack. This gave Joseph the excuse to send his servant after the men once they had departed.

A Fateful Discovery

The steward overtook the brothers very quickly and accused them of stealing the cup Joseph used for "divination" (v. 5). Now we should not assume that Joseph practiced any of the magic arts. This was part of Joseph's ploy to make it sound as though he were very Egyptian, and thus cast himself in an unfamiliar light in his brothers' eyes.

The brothers were so sure they were innocent of this theft that they pronounced a death sentence on the guilty party if anyone was found to have the cup. The steward settled for making the guilty one his slave and letting the others go free. We can imagine the outcry of the nine older brothers as the cup turned up in Benjamin's sack.

The brothers tore their clothes in anguish at the discovery. Then, according to verse 13, "they all loaded their donkeys and returned to the city" for what they assumed would be terrible consequences (vv. 13–14).

The Return to Egypt

We know they had not been gone very long because "Joseph was still in the house when Judah and his brothers came in" (v. 14). The first thing the men did upon appearing before Joseph was to throw themselves on the ground once again. This was getting to be a routine.

Judah spoke for the group, probably since he was the one who had guaranteed Benjamin's safety. "God has uncovered your servants' guilt," he said to Joseph (v. 16). Judah was expressing humility and remorse at the discovery of Joseph's cup among the brothers' possessions—an offense of which they were innocent.

But Judah's statement had a deeper ring of truth to it. God was orchestrating the events of their lives in such a way that their true guilt, their sin against Joseph, was now being uncovered. And Joseph had arranged events to test the depth of his brothers' repentance.

The story reached another dramatic climax when Joseph repeated the steward's sentence. "The man who was found to have the cup will become my slave. The rest of you, go back to your father in peace" (v. 17).

Can you see the irony in this situation? The ten brothers had thrown Joseph into the pit, then sold him to a caravan of traders, and then returned home, seemingly scot-free. Would they leave Benjamin in a similar predicament to save their own skins, going home and telling Jacob there was nothing they could do?

Judah's Second Offer

Not this time. Judah put himself on the line a second time for his baby brother. He approached Joseph and proceeded to deliver a heartrending plea, which included the offer to replace Benjamin as Joseph's slave so that Benjamin could go free. We will see that the speech moved Joseph to weep loudly and to make a startling revelation.

Judah's soliloquy is found in verses 18–34. It reveals the brothers' repentant attitude and Joseph's response.

Judah began by telling Joseph what he already knew, namely that Benjamin was especially beloved by his father because he was born to Jacob "in his old age." Besides, Judah continued, Benjamin's brother was dead, leaving Benjamin as the only surviving son of his mother, Rachel (vv. 18–20).

Joseph's heart must have wept as Judah recounted these details. All at once he was being confronted with memories of his father, his mother, Rachel, and the reminder of his own years of suffering. What a toll his supposed death must have taken on the family.

Judah then reminded Joseph of his warning to the brothers not to return to Egypt without their youngest brother and recounted the conversation that had ensued in Canaan when the food had run low (vv. 21–29).

Then Judah came to the crux of the issue: "If the boy is not with us when I go back to your servant my father and if my father, whose life is closely bound up with the boy's life, sees that the boy isn't there, he will die. Your servants will bring the gray head of our father down to the grave in sorrow" (vv. 30–31).

Judah felt the weight of this responsibility since, as we observed, it was he who had personally guaranteed Benjamin's safety (v. 32; cf. 43:8–10). So Judah made a proposal that signaled to Joseph the depth of the heart change that had occurred in his brother.

"Now then, please let your servant remain here as my lord's slave in place of the boy, and let the boy return with his brothers. How can I go back to my father if the boy is not with me? No! Do not let me see the misery that would come upon my father" (vv. 33–34).

Do you see the selflessness in this? This was a tremendous change of heart in Judah. Remember, this is the one who so many years before had been callously eating supper after tossing Joseph into the pit. As he ate, Judah had seen the traders coming and had suggested, "Hey, let's sell Joseph and make a few bucks" (see 37:26–27).

But this was not Judah trying to save his bacon. This was a contrite son saying, "I can't bear to bring my father any more pain. I can't bear to see him die in anguish. I've seen all of the agony we have caused him through our lies and intrigue, and I can't take it anymore. Please don't send me back home without Benjamin."

Joseph's Breaking Point

Throughout these meetings with his brothers, Joseph's overriding concern was for his father. He asked three times, "Is your father still living?" (see 43:7, 27; 45:3).

Amid all the emotions of this moment, it was Judah's appeal on behalf of his father that brought Joseph to the point at which he could no longer control his emotions (45:1–2). He not only broke down weeping, but his sobs were heard by the Egyptians, who relayed the message to Pharaoh, "Those Hebrew men have returned, and Joseph is weeping uncontrollably in his house."

A PICTURE OF JESUS

Notice Joseph's loving plea to his brothers, "Come close to me" (45:4).

I submit to you that this is an incredible response on Joseph's part. The meetings with his brothers had taken a deep emotional toll on him. He was reminded of all that they had done to him and of all the anguish they had put Jacob through for all of these years.

Joseph had the power to line his ten older brothers up against a wall and, with a measure of justification, order them to be cut down for their sins. He had the power to send these sinful ones to the grave on the strength of their rebellion, hatred, and animosity toward him.

But, instead, he reached out to them in love and forgiveness and said, "Come close to me."

What a wonderful picture of Jesus' response to you and me! We stood before Him in our sin and rebellion and animosity, completely condemned in His presence and utterly without excuse. We were deserving of death at His hands, yet Jesus went to the cross and took the death penalty we deserved.

And now He reaches out His hands, scarred by the nails of Calvary, and offers us forgiveness, salvation, and the wonder of a personal relationship with Himself. My dear reader, if you are unsure of your standing with God, I pray that you will flee to the outstretched hands of Jesus today!

Chapter Twelve

ONE
MOMENT
IN TIME

There are those moments in life when it seems that suddenly the clock stops and the action freezes. We know that, as a result of what we are experiencing, things will never be the same again.

Sometimes these moments in time are tied to a particular event. Many people can recall exactly where they were and what they were doing in November 1963 when the news came that President John Kennedy had been assassinated. Others have the same recollection of the January morning the space shuttle Challenger exploded in 1986, killing its seven astronauts.

There are also many personal moments in time for all of us: the birth of a child, the loss of a loved one, great moments of success, big changes in our lives. While they may not be known to everyone, these moments are frozen in time for us.

One of my moments was the day I arrived in America. It was August 3, 1983, and was a pivotal moment in time for me because I realized that nothing would ever be the same again. And, indeed, that has proved to be true.

Surely our friend Joseph, the governor of Egypt at this point in his pilgrimage, had such moments. When we get to heaven and ask Joseph, "In all that happened to you on the journey of your life, tell us what stood out the most to you," surely he will say, "One of those moments was when I disclosed myself to my brothers in Egypt."

This wonderful story recorded in Genesis 45 is one of the most dramatic moments in all the Bible. We can view these events from a number of angles.

A DEMONSTRATION OF HUMAN EMOTION

Let us note first that the opening verses of Genesis 45 depict a powerful demonstration of emotion, particularly on the part of Joseph.

Joseph's Emotional Struggle

This man had struggled with his emotions from the moment he saw his brothers standing in line to buy food. His feelings were especially strong the day Benjamin arrived in Egypt and the brothers came to Joseph's house for lunch (Genesis 43:30).

Joseph had to run out and find a place to weep. He must have wept quite a bit, too, because he had to wash the tears from his face and get control of himself before he could come back out and say something as simple as "Serve the food" (v. 31).

There were, no doubt, other occasions not recorded in which Joseph had to let go and give vent to his emotions. But apart from the exception noted above, he had managed to hold himself in check publicly. But all of that was about to change. The dam was about to burst. "Joseph could no longer control himself" and demanded to be left alone with his brothers (Genesis 45:1).

Joseph's Private Disclosure

The doors had no sooner closed on the twelve brothers than Joseph lost all semblance of composure. He began weeping so loudly that the Egyptians heard him, and someone even told Pharaoh (v. 2).

It was in this setting that Joseph made the announcement,

"I am Joseph!" (v. 3). Now he was weeping from a heart of tenderness and forgiveness, for we will see that Joseph had a profound understanding of God's sovereign hand on his life.

But the brothers didn't know all of this yet, so being shut up alone with Joseph struck terror in their hearts. After all, this was the stern Egyptian official who had imprisoned Simeon and had held their lives in his hands for some time now.

But as they stood there wide-eyed, their palms perspiring, this enigmatic Egyptian prime minister began to cry. Not gentle little tears, either. This guy was weeping and wailing in a way that could be heard through the walls. And then Joseph revealed his identity to his brothers. It must have hit them like a bombshell.

It's interesting to me that Joseph made his revelation in private with his brothers. There are those times when family matters need to be addressed, and no one but family members need be present.

Joseph was actually protecting his brothers by doing things this way, guarding their reputation against the unnecessary public revelation of their cruelty toward him twenty-two years earlier. We wonder what Joseph's servants would have done had they found out that these Hebrew shepherds had treated their master so badly. So in dismissing the servants Joseph was doing everything in his power to save his brothers' reputation.

Some might be tempted to think what a great opportunity Joseph had to let the world know what bad characters his brothers were, and how he had suffered so unjustly at their hands. Why not just call everyone in and expose these guys for all of their hatred and cruelty toward him?

But Joseph didn't do that. He had the attitude the apostle Peter later described as a love that "covers over a multitude of sins" (1 Peter 4:8). It takes great wisdom and spiritual maturity to pass over old wounds and wrongs and extend forgiveness to the offender.

The Brothers' Realization

As Joseph's emotions burst the dam of his outward control, his brothers must have been stunned. And when he said, "I am Joseph! Is my father still living?" (v. 3), they must have been startled again.

We can imagine one of the men turning to the others and saying, "Did you hear that? Did he just speak in our language?" Up to that point, all of their exchanges with him had been through an interpreter. As part of disguising his identity, Joseph had not spoken to them in their own tongue. For all they knew, he was an Egyptian who didn't speak Hebrew.

The eleven brothers didn't have long to wonder, though, because Joseph quickly said, "Come close to me. . . . I am your brother Joseph, the one you sold into Egypt!" (v. 4).

Now they knew who he was, for who else would know that they had sold him into Egypt more than two decades earlier?

Small wonder the brothers were terrified. They were in the presence of the one whom they had hated with a passion, without a just cause. We can picture them looking hard at Joseph, perhaps as he removed his Egyptian headdress, trying to see past the changes that twenty-two years had brought, trying to determine whether this was indeed their brother.

Suddenly, they saw the resemblance. And the shame of what they had done must have swept over them, to say nothing of their terror at the thought of what Joseph might do to them in reprisal. But he had a far different purpose in mind.

AN ILLUSTRATION OF DIVINE PROVIDENCE

Our thesis from the outset of this book has been that Joseph is a wonderful, real-life illustration of the biblical doctrine of God's providence.

Through the events of his life Joseph understood that God sovereignly orders all things that come to pass and preserves the lives of His creatures for His purposes. This understanding framed Joseph's life, and we encounter it here in Genesis 45 (as we will later in Genesis 50) when we read that he put his broth-ers' minds at ease.

A Time for Everything

As Joseph called for his brothers to gather around him, he must have seen the distress and remorse and fear in their eyes. And so he said, "Do not be distressed and do not be angry with yourselves for selling me here, because it was to save lives that God sent me ahead of you" (Genesis 45:5).

What a powerful statement of divine providence! There is also ample mystery here for our minds to ponder. The truth of God's providential care does not mean that every detail of our lives will fit into neat categories so that our days flow along smoothly. Joseph's experience is proof that life seldom works that way.

But the Bible tells us in Ecclesiastes 3:1, "There is a time for everything, and a season for every activity under heaven." The writer is declaring the fact of the providential, overruling hand of God in all of life and in all of human history. Joseph under-stood divine providence well enough to respond to his brothers the way he did.

The Mystery of Providence

Here is the great mystery of God's hand in Joseph's life. You will recall that his brothers sold him into slavery in part to pre-vent the realization of his dream that they would one day bow down to him. In order to insure that that day would never come, they took matters into their own hands and committed an evil act for which they were responsible.

But God in His overruling providence used their evil be-havior to bring Joseph into the very position of authority be-fore which the brothers were obliged to bow.

You can stay up long into the night trying to figure these things out. Joseph must have thought these issues through many times. Whatever the case, he arrived at the conclusion that his brothers' hatred of him and his journey to Egypt were part of a larger plan, and he responded accordingly.

When people fall into bitterness and a desire for revenge they are forgetting providence—a view of God and His work that takes in more than our immediate circumstances.

This has not always been the case. In earlier days in this country, it was customary for people to talk about the happy providences of God. For example, the Civil War writings of Confederate General Stonewall Jackson, a committed believer, make frequent reference to God as providentially overruling in the war's circumstances according to His purpose.

Today men and women do not want to bow before the mysteries of God's providence. But Joseph knew that God was not taken by surprise when his brothers stripped him of his coat and threw him into the pit.

The Benefits of Providence

Joseph looked beyond the actions and reactions of men when he told his brothers, "It was to save lives that God sent me ahead of you" (Genesis 45:5). Then he added, "[God] made me father to Pharaoh, lord of his entire household and ruler of all Egypt" (v. 8). Joseph saw the hand of God in his benefits.

Humanly speaking, Pharaoh may have been responsible for Joseph's exalted position. But Joseph realized that his promotion truly came from the hand of God. Pharaoh could not have acted as he did had not God, in His grace and wisdom and providential care, inclined the king's heart toward Joseph (see Proverbs 21:1).

When you and I begin to depend upon divine providence in that way, we can endure our afflictions without undue complaint and experience our blessings without undue pride.

Think it out. Neither you nor I can draw our next breath without God's enabling. Do we really think it's because we own that postgraduate degree or because we are so clever in business that we enjoy the things we have? Without demeaning or denying our efforts, we must confess that ultimately it is God who provides these things according to His purpose and grace.

Providence and Human Evil

Joseph's understanding of God's providence in his life was expressed by a statement he repeated three times. "God sent me ahead of you" (vv. 5, 7). "It was not you who sent me here, but God" (v. 8).

It's important to note that this was Joseph speaking, not the brothers. Coming from them, a statement like this would have sounded like they were trying to shift the blame from themselves to God.

In other words, the brothers could have said, "Look, Joseph, it was God who did all this, not us. He sent you here, so we're not responsible for what we did. Don't you understand? All of this was God's providence."

Had that happened, Joseph's answer would have been, "Yes, I understand God's providence. But that doesn't mean you can evade responsibility for your actions." Indeed, later on Joseph said, "You intended to harm me" (Genesis 50:20).

The difficulty I just described by this hypothetical conversation is the interplay between God's good providence and the evil actions of human beings. Lawson puts it this way: "God was the first cause. [The brothers] were but instruments overruled by Him for the accomplishment of His own purposes."

In Joseph's case, it was the will of God both that Joseph should be brought to Egypt and that the evil actions of his brothers should be the means used.

There is even more mystery in this aspect of the doctrine of providence. Let me make a few key points that may help our understanding here.

First, we must understand that the nature of sin is not altered by the use God makes of it. Divine providence does not mean we can just go out and sin because, after all, God is overruling everything to His glory anyway.

This is the faulty argument Paul demolishes in Romans 6

when he says, "Shall we go on sinning so that grace may increase? By no means!" (vv. 1–2).

Here's a second point to consider. The will of God never contains permission for us to do that which runs contrary to His revealed will in the Bible. God's will does not sanction our sin.

Poison does not cease to be poison just because it may be part of a medicine that heals. Poison is still poison—and sin is still sin for which the sinner is responsible, even though God may choose to use that sin for the unfolding of His plan. God bears no blame for our sin.

The Purposes of Providence

This raises one more question we need to address. People often wonder why, if God is sovereign and in control of everything, He allows so much sin in the world.

The answer from the Scripture is, for His own glory. God knows what He is doing. He has dealt with sin at the Cross, and He is about to deal with sin when He banishes the Evil One into hell forever.

But, in the meantime, sin serves God's purposes. And since He is God, let us not raise our voices in protest. Lawson says, "God not only permits sin, but He makes use of it. No sinner can do any evil that God has not intended to use for the advancement of His own glory." We see this truth brilliantly illustrated in the case of Joseph.

Although God overrules human sin, no one can use providence as a cloak or an excuse for wickedness. John Calvin writes:

> I grant [that] thieves and murderers and other evildoers are the instruments of divine providence. And the Lord himself uses these to carry out the judgments that He has determined with Himself. Yet I deny that they can derive from this any excuse for their evil deeds. Why? Will they either involve God in the same inequity with themselves? Or will they cloak their own depravity with His justice? They can do neither. In their own con-

science
they are so convicted as to be unable to clear themselves. In themselves they so discover all evil, but in Him only the lawful use of their evil intent as to preclude the charge against God. Well and good, for He works through them.

All the evil in what happened to Joseph was the responsibility of his brothers. God was not contaminated because He determined to use their evil activities in order to achieve an overarching purpose He had for His servant.

Calvin concludes concerning this issue, "Away then with this dog-like impudence which can indeed bark at God's justice afar off, but cannot touch it."

Without wishing to be unkind, we must acknowledge to our shame that in the last twenty-five years, there have been far too many books written in the evangelical world that are nothing other than "dog-like impudence." It is an expression of the low view in which the greatness and wonder of God are held today that people feel they have the right to call into question His purity and holiness.

THREE BENEFITS OF PROVIDENCE

This discussion of providence is set against the background of Joseph's revelation of himself to His brothers. It is important that we understand providence, but it is also a source of blessing to discover that this doctrine provides these very practical benefits.

Comfort in Trouble

First, the doctrine of providence brings us comfort in the face of great difficulty and sorrow.

You and I cannot really go to sleep at night without a proper view of God's providence. Why? Because unless we believe God is in sovereign control over every detail of life, we will live in paralyzing fear of what the next phone call or the next knock on our door might bring.

Instead of living in fear, we can rest in the confidence that the God who knows when a sparrow falls is profoundly involved in our lives. He has made us the special objects of His love, so will He not look after us?

I don't have any doubt that Joseph slept as well in the dungeon as he slept in the palace because he knew that ultimately his exaltations and his deprivations came from the hand of God.

Security in the Face of Chaos

I don't need to tell you that we are living in days of increasing national and international chaos.

As I write these words, the crisis in Kosovo is the focus of world attention. NATO warplanes are pummeling the nation of Yugoslavia. Three-quarters of a million ethnic Albanian refugees are overwhelming the efforts of relief agencies to meet their needs.

But by the time you read these sentences, the conflict over Kosovo will be a historical footnote and the headlines focused on another international hot spot.

What are we to make of it all? Where can we find security in a world that seems ready to erupt in massive conflict at any moment?

The prophet Isaiah gives us the answer. "Surely the nations are like a drop in a bucket; they are regarded as dust on the scales (Isaiah 40:15).

If you have ever gone to one of those open-air farmers' markets where they weigh out the fresh produce for you, you can be sure that the scales being used are full of dust and dirt. Think of the fine dirt that covers potatoes. No one insists that the farmer dust his scales or wash the potatoes before weighing them out, because all that dust is not enough to move the scales. It's just there.

The nations of the earth are like that dust in the eyes of God—and He is our security! We are preoccupied with the wrong thing. In the absence of an understanding of God's providence, people live in terror of world rulers. But an awareness of God's sovereign control removes the terror.

If you doubt it, look at Isaiah 40:25: "'To whom will you compare me? Or who is my equal?' asks the Holy One." Answer: There is no one who can compare to God. No one is His equal.

Do you want to have security in a world that is upside down and anxious and chaotic and extremely dangerous? Bow down before the wonder of God's providence.

Humility in Success

Third, and finally, the wonderful truth of God's providence enables us to have humility in success, for it makes us aware that all of our successes are gifts from God.

Joseph said of God, "He made me father to Pharaoh" (Genesis 45:8). He knew who had made him second-in-command in Egypt.

An awareness of providence enables us to treat others with humility—even those who have injured or wronged us. When we recognize that God is ultimately in control of our circumstances, we can release others and their actions to Him and be free of the bitterness and resentment that rots the soul. Joseph's profound understanding of providence was the key to his attitude toward his brothers and, indeed, toward life itself.

𝒜
LESSON IN
FORGIVENESS

As the hand of God fashions Joseph's life according to His sovereign purposes, we see Joseph's godly character emerging like a diamond revealing new facets with every turn.

One such facet of this amazing story is the genuine forgiveness Joseph extended to his brothers. What do you think they were expecting to hear after he finally told them, "I am Joseph!" (Genesis 45:3)?

The Bible says they were terrified. I'm sure they didn't imagine that he was going to follow up that announcement by saying, "Do not be distressed and do not be angry with yourselves for selling me here" (v. 5).

Such a blanket statement of forgiveness must have stunned Joseph's brothers. To be honest, it strikes *us* as strange. After all, shouldn't people who have sinned as grievously as these characters be made aware of their guilt and have time to grieve over their actions? Was Joseph just brushing aside the wrong done to him twenty-two years earlier? Was he saying, "It doesn't really matter"?

THE NEED FOR FORGIVENESS

That's not what Joseph was doing. He had already discovered through his testing of them that his brothers had repentant hearts, a process he could see was underway in their admission of guilt (Genesis 42:21).

Joseph wept on that occasion, I believe, because he realized his brothers were actually coming to an acknowledgment of their sin previously. When he had no reason to believe they were facing up to their guilt, he had treated them with severity so that they might be awakened to their sinfulness.

Similarly, that is why the law of God is preached to us, that we might be brought to an awareness of our sin and guilt and be moved to repentance and faith.

In Joseph's case, when he realized that his brothers were deeply humbled and overwhelmed with guilt and confusion, he was concerned that they not carry their grief to excess. Their crime was not too great to be forgiven by God, or by Joseph.

The same is true for us. Our sins are not too great to be forgiven by God, or by the brother or the sister we have offended.

The fact is, it is sometimes much easier to forgive the injuries done to us than to believe that the injuries we have caused are forgiven. I spend a lot of time in pastoral counseling trying to assure people that when God says that He "will remember their sins no more" (Jeremiah 31:34), He means exactly what He says.

It is not that Joseph let the brothers off the hook or gave them some easy way out so they didn't have to answer for their hatred and jealousy of him. It is that having seen their repentance, he didn't want them to be buried with undue sorrow.

Having forgiven the men, Joseph threw his arms around Benjamin's neck and wept, and Benjamin hugged Joseph and wept also (Genesis 45:14). That's understandable, because these two were full brothers. Benjamin hadn't been involved in hating Joseph and wanting to kill him.

But then Joseph reached out and "kissed all his brothers and wept over them" (v. 15). He kissed those ten men who had wished him dead and were now at his mercy. Joseph's kiss was not a Judas kiss of betrayal, but a kiss of complete forgiveness.

So let us face the question: Can we kiss all our brothers and sisters, whether physical or spiritual, the way Joseph kissed his brothers? Or are we still holding grudges over things that are microscopic compared to what Joseph went through?

If so, it could be that we don't understand the true nature of forgiveness. Or the reason may be that we have made the choice to turn off the path of righteousness, and now our wheels are in the ditch. If we are harboring unforgiveness toward someone, we'll find that we cannot worship or witness, and our usefulness in the kingdom of God is sadly diminished.

Consider the words of Jesus from the cross: "Father, forgive them, for they do not know what they are doing" (Luke 23:34). Can we who have been forgiven every debt by God honestly tell Him we plan to hold a grudge against our brother and sister the rest of our lives over what might be some marginal, minimal offense?

Of all things, the church is to be the people of forgiveness. Is that not part of the prayer our Lord taught us to pray? "Forgive us our debts, as we also have forgiven our debtors" (Matthew 6:12).

If we were to ask people what they consider the hardest things to say to someone else, I suspect that two recurring answers would be, "I am sorry," and "I forgive you." Our pride is so great that we are reluctant to admit to being wrong; and perhaps even sadder, we are slow to grant forgiveness to those who seek it from us.

As Archbishop Temple has said, "To return evil for good is devilish. To return good for good is human. To return good for evil is divine." Forgiveness is not some little extra part of Christian experience; it is at the very heart of it. These events in Joseph's life demand that we grapple with the implications in our lives.

AN ILLUSTRATION OF FORGIVENESS

There is so much that is striking about the account before us in Genesis 45. Joseph forgave not in word only, but also in deed. Consider what he did for the brothers who had mistreated him so cruelly.

Simply put, the events of Genesis 45 are an amazing illustration of Joseph's forgiving heart.

Joseph's brothers had driven him as far away from them as they could. But when it was his turn to be in control, he said, "Come close to me" (v. 4).

Joseph's brothers had sent him off as a captive to Egypt on the back of a mangy camel. But he gave them fine Egyptian carts for their journey home (v. 21).

Joseph's brothers were willing to leave him to die of thirst and starvation in the pit. But he gave them provisions for the trip back to Canaan (v. 21).

Joseph's brothers had torn his clothes off, but he gave them clothes (v. 22).

Joseph's brothers had sold him for money, but he gave Benjamin three hundred shekels of silver (v. 22). Joseph even gave his brothers wise counsel, knowing their tendencies. "Don't quarrel on the way!" (v. 24).

Do you see what is happening here? Joseph returned their every evil, cruel, and merciless acts with goodness and kindness and mercy. Centuries before Paul's words were ever written, Joseph was a living illustration of the admonition, "'If your enemy is hungry, feed him; if he is thirsty, give him something to drink.' . . . Do not be overcome by evil, but overcome evil with good" (Romans 12:20–21; see also Matthew 5:44–48).

Jesus revolutionizes lives by His forgiveness in order that forgiven lives might be revolutionary in their impact. This is the impact the church is to make on the world. We're supposed to be the forgiving ones. But do you think conservative evangelicalism is viewed by the rank and file of people in the United States as an example of this kind of revolutionary forgiveness?

Not a chance. We're known as the protesters, the sign wavers, the shouters—and even, sometimes, the shooters. Our culture has us pegged as a special interest group. We have been placed in a neat little economic and political pigeonhole. And we have largely done it to ourselves by trying to make our impact in the economic and political arenas at the expense of kingdom living.

Jesus did not come to set up a political or economic kingdom. Of course, there are justifiable concerns in the culture that we must address. And sometimes that requires taking an adversarial role. But have you ever considered what would happen if we really tried to overcome evil with good? If we took the time and personnel and money and resources at our disposal to open our hearts and homes to drug addicts, to AIDS victims, and to girls who are pregnant without wanting to be, the impact would be incredible.

If we start on an individual basis to transform our streets and our culture, when people drive down the street they will say, "See that house? Those people took in three pregnant girls, and they're taking care of them. Can you believe it? It's amazing what's happening in that house."

That is letting your light shine before men in such a way that they will praise your Father in heaven (see Matthew 5:16). That is exactly what was happening in Genesis 45. The brothers saw the carts, clothes, and cash Joseph provided. They heard his counsel. And they headed home no doubt mystified that they, who had offended their brother so greatly, should be on the receiving end of such dramatic, tangible forgiveness.

AN EXPLANATION OF FORGIVENESS

Joseph provides a wonderful illustration of Christlike forgiveness. Fast forward for a moment to Matthew 18 where we discover Jesus providing crucial principles on the subject in response to a question by Peter.

The Mistake of Moralism

In Matthew, Peter was thinking like a moralist when he asked Jesus the question, "Lord, how many times shall I forgive my brother when he sins against me? Up to seven times?" (Matthew 18:21).

That's a good question. We can imagine Peter thinking so, too, and being quite proud of it. Maybe he was expecting a pat on the back from Jesus for wanting to forgive his brother, especially since Peter was ready to be so generous about it.

But Peter was really saying, "Lord, I know I'm supposed to forgive people more than just once. I wanted to put their names on my list and check off the times I have forgiven them, so that I can take care of them after that. I was wondering if seven times would be enough?"

One of the dangers in teaching about the need for forgiveness is that someone will respond to the Bible's message at the level of moralism.

Here's how a moralist might respond to Joseph's forgiveness of his brothers. "What a wonderful example. You know, I've been an irreligious sort of person. I haven't really lived by the Golden Rule. But recently, I have plugged back into religion, and I'm trying to find out what I'm supposed to do.

"So what I hear you telling me is that I need to be a forgiving person. Fine, I'm going to try very hard to do that, starting right now. I'll let you know how I'm getting on."

That's the mistake of moralism, a misunderstanding of what we're talking about. Moralism is merely an external attempt at reform. It is not the gospel. But people are listening to this kind of teaching every Sunday in many churches and then going out and trying to be the right kind of people in their own strength.

A Matter of the Heart

But Jesus told Peter, "I tell you, not seven times, but seventy-seven times" (v. 22; some versions say "seventy times seven"). Whatever the number, that's not the issue, because forgiveness is not a matter of calculation. It's a matter of the heart.

You don't forgive your husband or wife or children on the basis on how many times you've forgiven them on a certain day, do you? Jesus' response is a picture of unlimited forgiveness.

Jesus was saying, "Peter, if you understood forgiveness you would not be asking if you could limit it to seven times." Then Jesus told a story to explain what the forgiveness of the kingdom of heaven is like (vv. 23–35).

The story involves a king who was settling accounts with his servants. A man was brought before the king who owed him an incalculable amount of money. The man could not pay, but pled for mercy, and the king forgave him the entire debt.

Then this servant went out and found a chap who owed him a few dollars. When he couldn't give it to him, the servant started choking him and demanding that he pay up. The poor man begged for time to pay the debt, but the unforgiving servant refused and had the man thrown into prison.

When the king was told what had happened, he brought the forgiven servant back and said, "I canceled all that debt of yours because you begged me to. Shouldn't you have had mercy on your fellow servant just as I had on you?" (vv. 32–33). Then the king had the man imprisoned and tortured for his unbelievable lack of forgiveness.

Lessons in Forgiveness

The lesson of Matthew 18 is this: Prompted by gratitude, forgiven sinners must always do everything in their power to forgive whoever has offended them and to bring about complete reconciliation.

There are a number of factors to be considered which are absolutely crucial in understanding the nature of forgiveness. Indeed, we will never know what it is either to be forgiven or to forgive apart from understanding these truths. Let me give them to you in summary fashion.

1. *We are all God's debtors.* "All have sinned and fall short of the glory of God" (Romans 3:23). We have all missed the mark, in terms of the target of His righteousness. If you doubt that, read the Ten Commandments and see if you can get past number one without having to acknowledge that you have fouled it up.

2. *We cannot do anything to repay our debt.* Paul says in Romans 3:20, "No one will be declared righteous in [God's] sight by observing the law; rather, through the law we become conscious of sin."

This is why moralism doesn't work. External religion is sending people to hell because they think that by doing good things, they can repay the debt and be acceptable in God's sight. But that's as absurd as the servant in Jesus' story trying to pay back his impossible debt to the king.

3. *By means of Christ's atoning sacrifice, the debt has been paid for all who believe in Him.* First we must see the bad news that we're all in debt to God. Then comes worse news: There is no way we can get ourselves out of debt. But the good news is that Someone has done something on our behalf so as to make possible a radical transformation in our circumstances.

Romans 3:24 says, "[We] are justified freely by his grace through the redemption that came by Christ Jesus." When Jesus died on the cross, He was not simply offering us a nice example of selflessness. He was paying our sin debt.

This is crucial to grasp because many people want to sentimentalize the gospel. "Look what those horrible people did to that nice man Jesus," they say. "Maybe I should do something for Jesus. Maybe if I go to church, Jesus will see me and be happy; then He'll take me to His eternal church."

So driven by sentimentalism, people respond in moralism and hope to end up in heaven—and it's never going to happen. We are hopelessly in debt to God, and our only hope is the wonderful news that "God made him [Jesus] who had no sin to be sin for us, so that in him we might become the righteousness of God" (2 Corinthians 5:21). This is the gospel. This is what we must believe and accept in order to be saved and have our debt to God canceled.

4. *We must forgive the debts of those who are indebted to us in order to experience the assurance of our forgiveness.* Now don't get this the wrong way around. We saw earlier that Jesus teaches us to pray, "Forgive us our debts, as we also have forgiven our debtors" (Matthew 6:12).

Most people think this means that if we forgive other people their debts against us, God will then forgive our debt. But that's not the meaning here. Rather, it is in our forgiveness of other people's sins against us that we *reveal* the fact that we have been forgiven by God.

That's the message of Matthew 18. The ungrateful servant didn't understand forgiveness. He didn't appreciate the enormity of the debt from which he was released. Otherwise, he would never have tried to choke the life out of the chap who owed him a few dollars.

Joseph didn't have all the doctrinal formulations about forgiveness to go by. But his treatment of his brothers illustrates that he understood the doctrine of forgiveness in a profound way.

5. *It should not be too difficult for those who have been forgiven to forgive in turn.* The reason is that what we owe God is infinitely more than what any person owes us.

The key here is to understand how utterly bankrupt we are before God. If I live my life thinking I'm really quite a good person and that, frankly, God should be gratified at the prospect of having me in His group; if I never understand myself to be spiritually bankrupt, then I will hold all kinds of grudges against people.

That's one of the ways in which the self-esteem movement works against the message of the gospel. The prevailing emphasis of our culture is to tell people that what's wrong with them is that they feel bad about themselves. If they will just feel better about themselves, they can be cured of anything.

But the Bible says you'll never feel good about yourself until you learn first to feel bad about yourself. When you realize how bad things really are, then you are in a position to learn how to feel truly good. Then it won't be about you, but about the One who died to forgive your great debt so that you, in turn, can be a debt forgiver to others around you.

Anytime I harbor animosity toward anyone, it is because I have diminished my sense of the debt I owe to the living God.

6. *The unforgiving person is destined for everlasting punishment.* As we have said, it is the forgiving person who gives evidence of having been forgiven. And since it is only those who have been forgiven who will live in heaven with Jesus, if I am unforgiving I reveal myself as unforgiven and, therefore, someone destined to dwell in a Christless eternity.

7. *Both the offender and the offended should take steps toward reconciliation.* If we are truly forgiven people, we will have a forgiving spirit toward others no matter which side of an offense we happen to find ourselves on.

THE APPLICATION OF FORGIVENESS

We are confronted by two simple questions in light of what we're learning.

Question number one is this: Have you ever acknowledged

the enormity of your sin and responded to God's invitation to come close to Him and be forgiven? Have you faced your bankrupt condition before God and thrown yourself on His mercy? I trust you have.

Now for question number two: If you have been forgiven by God, are you then taking seriously Jesus' instruction to forgive others from your heart, without limitation?

Jesus said, "By this all men will know that you are my disciples, if you love one another" (John 13:35). When we love one another, we must forgive one another. Forgiveness is the classic illustration of genuine love.

So what must we do about forgiveness? Let's do what is necessary for genuine forgiveness to take place. Let's not become hypocritical pretenders, who kiss and hug and smile and say everything is fine when it isn't.

Forgiveness needs to come from our hearts. It needs to be the kind of genuine, soul-searching, gut-wrenching, experiential forgiveness that doesn't keep a record of wrongs committed (see 1 Corinthians 13:5).

When we come to confess a wrong against a brother or sister and seek forgiveness, it is important to remember that the circle of confession need be no larger than the circle of the offense.

That means we don't have to go around confessing to people every wrong thought we have ever had about them. That will only cause embarrassment and needless offense, and may actually aggravate the situation we are trying to resolve.

If the sin remains secret in the mind and does not erupt into words or deeds against the other person, it must be confessed to God alone. The rule is always that secret sins must be confessed secretly to God, and private sins must be confessed privately to the injured party.

Forgiveness is not a shallow, "Oh, it's OK. Forget it." Genuine forgiveness like that which Joseph expressed toward his brothers is a heart-changing experience.

The church of Jesus Christ is a community of the imperfect, and therefore it is a community in which there is need for
forgiveness among the members. Let us take Joseph's example
to heart, going and doing likewise.

Chapter Fourteen

𝒜
PILGRIM'S
PROGRESS

Genesis 46–47 contain at least four crucial, dramatic scenes that capture the action and take us the next few steps in the unfolding of this incredible story of God's providence.

The primary character in this portion of the drama is Jacob rather than Joseph, but it's important that we follow Jacob at this point because he is about to move to Egypt and be reunited with Joseph. These events also trace God's hand at work in Joseph's life.

JACOB WAS STUNNED BY EVENTS

Scene one begins at the end of Genesis 45. Jacob's sons returned from Egypt and informed him, "Joseph is still alive! In fact, he is ruler of all Egypt (v. 26).

"Jacob was stunned; he did not believe them" (v. 26). After more than twenty years of believing Joseph to be dead, this news was too much for Jacob to process.

Confused by What He Heard

We don't know if the brothers simply rushed in and blurted out their announcement with no warning, or whether there was some sort of preamble to this stunning news that is not recorded in the Scripture.

We can imagine the confusion in Jacob's mind at this point. As far as he was concerned, the death of Joseph was the most wrenching event of the past two decades. It must have taken him a long time to reconcile himself to the idea that his beloved boy, whom he had watched go off that day as a seventeen-year-old, was not coming home.

If you had asked Jacob, he would have been able to describe the events of that day with all the passion of a father's heart. He could have told of his anticipation that Joseph would be home before too long and yet of his awareness of the dangers of the trip. He could have told you what it had been like to wave to Joseph until he was beyond the horizon and out of sight.

You may know that many of the rail platforms in Britain are very long. The trains start off slowly, and you can wave good-bye to your loved one for quite a while. But once the train disappears, you won't see the person, no matter how long you stand there.

I suspect that's what it had been like for Jacob as he watched Joseph disappear over the horizon. And then he had waited for Joseph to come home, but he never came.

And now, twenty-two years later, the same characters who had brought Joseph's torn, bloodstained coat to Jacob were standing before him telling him his son was alive. No wonder he was stunned. He had two decades worth of information stored in the computer of his mind telling him Joseph was dead. He just couldn't process the new information. Then, while he was trying to come to terms with the fact that Joseph was alive, his sons added a second, equally indigestible layer to the information cake he was struggling to swallow. "He is ruler of all Egypt" (v. 26).

Can't you just see him trying to grapple with this inexplicable mystery?

As the boys unfolded their tale of Joseph's kindness and his instructions to bring the family to Egypt, Jacob reeled in unbelief. But then they took him outside and showed him the carts laden with the goods Joseph had sent with them.

Convinced by What He Saw

If what Jacob heard confused him, what he saw convinced him. His driveway was filled with carts and donkeys loaded down with good things, and he knew they didn't belong to him.

Furthermore, these carts weren't Canaanite carts. The steering wheels were on the wrong side, if you like. Their markings and features told Jacob these were foreign carts.

Jacob surveyed the scene and it suddenly sank in that what his sons were telling him was true. "I'm convinced!" he cried out. "My son Joseph is still alive. I will go and see him before I die" (Genesis 45:28).

JACOB WAS STRENGTHENED BY GOD

In scene two Jacob, as the head of a large and hungry family, sets out for Egypt "with all that was his" (Genesis 46:1), eager to see Joseph again.

His caravan stopped at a place called Beersheba, rich with significance for Jacob's family. In Genesis 21:33 Jacob's grandfather Abraham planted a tamarisk tree in Beersheba after making a treaty with Abimelech; there Abraham had called on the name of the Lord.

Jacob's father Isaac had also stopped at Beersheba. He had built an altar, called on the name of the Lord, and had his servants dig a well (26:23–25). So, on his own journey, Jacob purposefully stopped at Beersheba and built an altar of sacrifice to God.

The Attitude He Revealed

First, by offering sacrifices to God, Jacob revealed that he knew himself to be a sinner in need of pardon.

Every time the patriarchs offered sacrifices, they were acknowledging their offenses before God and their hope of forgiveness through the better sacrifice that would one day come—which we know to be the Lamb of God, who takes away the sin of the world.

The others traveling with Jacob must have wondered why he was stopping at Beersheba when so much was waiting for him in Egypt. Wasn't Jacob eager to see his son Joseph again?

He was, but Jacob stopped because he was a worshiper. And worshipers worship. Jacob didn't need anyone to tell him it was time to do this. He built an altar and offered sacrifices to God because he knew he was a sinner in need of pardon and a pilgrim in need of guidance.

There is another reason Jacob sought out God at this particular point in his pilgrimage. Again, we must turn back to Genesis 26 for the context. In verse 2 of that chapter we read that God appeared in a vision to Isaac and specifically commanded him not to go to Egypt.

Because Jacob was aware of that command he would be concerned lest his desire to be reunited with Joseph put him in a place of disobedience to God. For Jacob, even the passionate concerns of family were subservient to the clear mandate of God.

Jacob was affirming that no matter how excited he was about seeing Joseph, a good conscience toward God was ultimately more important than seeing his son again. Jacob allowed eternity to so fill his mind that time took its proper place. Like Jacob, we too will benefit from reminding ourselves that we are

- sinners in need of pardon,
- worshipers of the one true God, and
- pilgrims in need of guidance.

The Assurance He Received

Look at the assurance Jacob received in response to the attitude he displayed.

God spoke to Jacob in a night vision. "I am God, the God of your father. . . . Do not be afraid to go down to Egypt, for I will make you into a great nation there. I will go down to Egypt with you, and I will surely bring you back again. And Joseph's own hand will close your eyes" (Genesis 46:3–4).

Why did God identify Himself as "the God of your father"? He did so because He was saying, "Jacob, I was faithful to your father, Isaac, all the days of his life, and I will be faithful to you."

God's promise to make a great nation out of Jacob's family must have seemed far-fetched to this clan. They were only some seventy people (vv. 26–27) fleeing their home during a famine and traveling to a foreign land in a bunch of borrowed carts, wearing used clothes and accompanied by some donkeys and a few other bits and pieces.

But God wasn't looking just at the immediate circumstances of Jacob. He was fulfilling the promise He had made to Abraham many years before that his offspring would be "like the dust of the earth" in number (Genesis 13:16).

This is the great wonder of God's dealings with us. Who are we, what are we, and what do we have to offer God? Nothing. What do we have to say? Nothing. So unless He strengthens us and assures of His presence, we had better stay where we are. But when God does speak, then we may go boldly.

The picture of Jacob's entourage is almost comical. They must have looked like "The Beverly Hillbillies" some four thousand years B.C. The people in Canaan were saying, "Where ya goin', Jake?"

He replied, "We're heading to Egypt. My boy's a millionaire. He's head of the whole shebang down there. He wants us to come to him. That's why we have these new carts with the steering wheels on the wrong side. Look at Benjamin. He's got all these clothes and silver. It's unbelievable."

So the caravan rolled on toward Egypt, and with each turn of the carts' wheels the anticipation mounted. Jacob was on his way to see Joseph!

As fathers, we can surely identify with the feelings that must have been stirring within Jacob's heart. Having been gone for a while, we know the sensation of checking our watch again and again as we anticipate the end of our journey and the prospect of reunion.

Jacob must have been feeling those same stirrings when suddenly on the horizon appears a cloud of dust. Jacob strains his eyes to look into the distance and sees a chariot coming his way. As the entourage draws near, Jacob sees Joseph, and in an instant they are together. Eyes meeting, arms reaching, locked in an impassioned embrace, the tears of love dampening the shoulders of each man. There is little doubt that is the crowning moment of Jacob's earthly pilgrimage. Over twenty years of his life are squeezed into this hug. Past sorrows are forgotten, past evil deeds forgiven.

JACOB WAS SATISFIED WITH LIFE

Seeing Joseph alive and well was so incredible that Jacob was able to say, "Now I am ready to die, since I have seen for myself that you are still alive" (v. 30).

Satisfied in the Puzzle of Life

Jacob was satisfied even though his life, like ours, was often a puzzle to him. We often have no explanation for life's disappointments, failures, and even its joys. But can we look at all of that and say, "I am satisfied," in face of the puzzles? Yes. As the workings of God's providence become ever more real to us, as we look back and realize that He has been preparing us for the present day we can say, "Father, I am satisfied in You, even though life is often a puzzle to me."

Seeing Joseph after more than two decades of separation and sadness did not answer all of Jacob's questions, but the patriarch was no longer worried about them. He was content as he learned to leave God to order all his ways and trust Him whatever happened.

Satisfied in the Prospect of Death

Jacob's statement that he was ready to die was not a death wish. It was an expression of a satisfaction that sounds strange today in a world caught up in the pursuit of meaning and materialism on this side of the grave.

Satisfaction in the face of death is grounded in something far deeper than anything Earth can provide. It's the satisfaction toward which the psalmist looked when he said to God, "In righteousness I will see your face; when I awake, I will be satisfied with seeing your likeness" (Psalm 17:15).

The apostle John says, "When he appears, we shall be like him, for we shall see him as he is" (1 John 3:2). Why do we let our hearts reside in a world of dissatisfaction when we have so much to enjoy? It's because we are seeking our satisfaction in things that were never designed to produce it and, indeed, are incapable of doing so.

Mick Jagger, of the Rolling Stones rock music group, sang in the sixties, "I can't get no satisfaction." In the nineties, Jagger was no more satisfied than he was thirty years before because he was still heading down dead-end streets looking for the answer.

I once asked a group of stockbrokers if they knew if many of their clients were contented. You'd have thought I had asked them a brainteaser, because the silence was deafening. They looked at each other and decided that among them they did not know of a single client who was truly content.

Jacob looked beyond the puzzles of life to the prospect of death and said, "I am satisfied." Can we say the same?

JACOB WAS SETTLED IN GOSHEN

The fourth and final scene was played out as Jacob and his family arrived in the area of Goshen, where he was reunited with Joseph (Genesis 46:28–30). Two aspects of these events in particular reveal God's hand of providence in the life of Jacob.

The Prime Site

When Jacob and his family arrived from Canaan, Joseph outlined for them exactly what they should say to Pharaoh (46:31–34). Joseph knew how Pharaoh would respond, and Joseph wanted the best for his father Jacob—and that included seeing to it that Pharaoh settled Jacob and his family in the best part of Egypt.

Now there's a kind of perversity that would say that Joseph shouldn't have put his dad in the best place, for that would be selfish. But Joseph's actions were a testimony to the Lord's goodness and to his affection for his father. You do your best for your parents. Joseph said, "Dad, I have a great place for you." God gives all things richly to enjoy.

Joseph is a wonderful example of providing for one's family. His life reminds us that we should use every opportunity to repay the kindness and love of our parents. It is unnatural to fail at this point.

For twenty-two years Joseph had been separated from Jacob, unable to do anything for him. Now he had the chance to provide the best of Egypt for his father, and he seized the moment.

We can imagine Joseph telling Jacob, "Let me show you where you're going to live. Look at this view; look at the house I've built for you. Isn't this nice, Dad?"

Thank God for every example of children who care for their parents. May God forgive those of us who are stingy toward our parents. Think of all of their sacrifices for us. Wouldn't it be the greatest joy of life to sacrifice for them?

The care that we take of our parents in their old age is an expression of godliness (1 Timothy 5:8). So we're told in Genesis 47:11, "Joseph settled his father and his brothers in Egypt and gave them property in the best part of the land." Joseph was delighted to settle his dad in a prime site.

Jacob's Pilgrim Status

When Joseph brought Jacob in to meet Pharaoh, Jacob readily acknowledged his pilgrim status before the Egyptian ruler. "The years of my pilgrimage are a hundred and thirty" (v. 9).

In other words, Jacob was giving evidence that he was not bound by the stuff of Earth. He was saying, "This is a nice place Joseph has given me, but I'm not staying here. I'm on my way to the place of my fathers."

The way in which you and I respond to our "prime site" of life shows the extent to which we understand our pilgrim status. Many people who come to their version of Goshen fall in love with the place so much they get all tied up in it and start living like they're going to be there forever.

There is a distinct difference between living for time and living for eternity. Although Jacob was surely not around when it was written he would have gladly sung the song, "This world is not my home, I'm just a-passing through. My treasures are laid up, somewhere beyond the blue."

When you're living in a good spot and things are going well, it's hard not to get trapped in materialism. But sometimes, in a moment of wonder, the light of eternity breaks into the experience of time. The inrush of heaven floods our souls. These are precious moments we need to hold on to, for they remind us that this place in which we are living is not the end. We're just passing through on our pilgrim journey to heaven.

How do we explain our preoccupation with the *now?* Because we've lost sight of the *then.* Why are we consumed with the prospect of getting everything fixed politically down here? Because we perhaps have lost sight of heaven. Why are we trying to make the United States the perfect place to live? Because perhaps we've determined this is the *only* place we're going to live.

When we were kids, we used to go camping. Our guide would take us on treks into the hills. The living was rugged. No toilets or anything else. It was absolutely pathetic, dreadful.

The guide would say, "When we get to the top of this hill, it's going to be wonderful."

As one of the more positive members of the group, I would say things like, "Yeah, well, it better be, because this is horrible."

I mention this because one of the songs the camping leader taught us to sing went like this:

A few more marchings weary, then we'll gather home.
A few more storm clouds dreary, then we'll gather home.
O'er time's rapid river soon we'll rest forever.
A few more marchings weary, and then we'll gather home!

This is the progress of a pilgrim. May we put our feet in the footprints that pilgrims like Jacob have left for us.

As a pilgrim who knew that he was moving on, Jacob was also concerned about the blessing of his grandchildren. In Genesis 48, Jacob reminded Joseph of God's blessing on his life, and then the patriarch proceeded to bless Joseph's two sons in light of that blessing.

How significant was this? When the writer of Hebrews came to describe an incident from the life of Jacob that was representative of his faith, what did he choose? Not Jacob's wrestling with the angel, or his journey to Egypt, but his blessing of Joseph's sons. "By faith Jacob, when he was dying, blessed each of Joseph's sons, and worshiped as he leaned on the top of his staff" (Hebrews 11:21).

The significance of what we might be tempted to regard as a minor detail is found in the fact that Jacob was revealing to his posterity the fact that God had plans and purposes for them. He was declaring anew his faith in the certainty of God's promises. For you see, the promises were only good if God's word proved to be true. Jacob was convinced that God was true to His word and that the land promised to him would be given to him and his descendants.

This was the pilgrimage of Jacob. After seventeen years in Egypt, Jacob blessed his grandsons, then "drew his feet up into the bed, breathed his last and was gathered to his people" (Genesis 49:33). Joseph and his brothers took Jacob back to Canaan for burial in accordance with his wishes (Genesis 50:1–13). The pilgrim had finally come home to stay.

Chapter Fifteen

✠FTER
THE FUNERAL

The death of a family member is one of the hardest events any of us will have to face. The loss of a loved one can send shock waves through a family, especially when that individual has been the head of the family over a significant number of years, as was Jacob.

When that important family member is gone, a number of things happen, not the least of which is that family relationships are often shown for what they really are. A crisis such as a death does not create situations so much as it reveals them. A death in the family quickly exposes what the members of that family really believe and how they really behave.

After years of dealing with grieving families, it is clear to me that usually it is not until after the funeral service that the true family issues, concerns, and conflicts come to the surface. Many times I discover that it was only custom or good manners that allowed a particular family to display unity during the mourning for a family member.

But soon after the funeral has been held and the daily routine has returned, family grievances that have been repressed, old wounds that have never been treated, and poisons that have never been purged begin to surface.

Given all that we know of Joseph's family, it's hardly surprising that the death of Jacob brought to the fore old fears and buried animosities. Joseph's brothers were about to reveal something of what had been going on in their hearts.

THE FEARS OF JOSEPH'S BROTHERS

The revelation of what was in their hearts came in the form of a question they asked each other. "When Joseph's brothers saw that their father was dead, they said, 'What if Joseph holds a grudge against us and pays us back for all the wrongs we did to him?'" (Genesis 50:15).

There's a sense in which this concern on the part of the brothers was not surprising. Even after seventeen years of living in prosperity in Egypt under Joseph's kind hand, the brothers would have been less than human if the thought of possible revenge did not cross their minds. But it is clear from the text that this was more than simply a passing thought. All the time they had been living in Egypt they had harbored the fear that Joseph was just waiting to crush them for the evil they had done to him.

An Ill-Founded Fear

This fear was based on the assumption that the only restraining factor in Joseph's life, the one thing that had kept him from taking his vengeance, was the presence of Jacob. Joseph's brothers feared that once Jacob was gone, there was no saying what Joseph might do to them. With Jacob in the grave, Joseph would be free to repay them.

As I read this Scripture passage, I find myself wondering why the brothers thought this way after Joseph had forgiven them and done so much for them.

One reason might have been that the brothers knew that this was the way things normally worked in the world. The majority of people who had been treated as cruelly as Joseph would have seized the opportunity for revenge as soon as it presented itself. That has been the common practice throughout history.

A second reason the brothers might have had for fearing that Joseph would take revenge was that that was what they themselves would have done if the situation had been reversed. We tend to assign to others the motives and attitudes we harbor in our own hearts. Joseph's brothers attributed to him the evil they would have carried out if the roles had been reversed.

But what would prove far more painful to Joseph would be if his brothers' fears revealed that they did not fully believe him when he forgave them so many years before. Seventeen full years had passed since the family's arrival in Canaan, and still they did not trust Joseph (cf. 47:9, 28).

Did the brothers believe that Joseph had been playing the hypocrite for all those years?. Or if they assumed that his earlier forgiveness was real, the passing of time had caused him to change his mind? For whatever reason, Joseph's brothers did not feel forgiven, and they had apparently been in deep turmoil about it for a number of years.

What If?

Does this scenario sound familiar to you? The predicament of these brothers is similar to what many people go through with respect to their salvation. Before we proceed with the account in Genesis 50, we need to stop and consider the problem we might call the "What if?" syndrome.

Although they might have come to Jesus years before in repentance and faith and were welcomed by Him and caught up in His embrace, many people still ask regularly such questions as "What if it wasn't real?" "What if I'm not forgiven?" "What if I'm not going to heaven?" "What if God's promises are faulty?"

Such questions never cross some people's minds. But, for others, and I suspect it is a significant company, these experiences of doubt and misgiving are frequent. These thoughts come in large measure because people do not submit what they feel emotionally to the reality of what they know intellectually.

Martin Luther knew something of this when he wrote,

"For feelings come and feelings go, now feelings are deceiving. My warrant is the word of God, not else is worth believing. Though all my heart should feel condemned for want of some sweet token, there is One greater than my heart whose Word cannot be broken."

If Joseph's brothers had been genuinely repentant of their sin seventeen years earlier, God would not come back to punish them later. But they might have condemned and, in some degree, punished themselves through living in the fear of "What if?"

The answer to this problem is given in a letter on Christian assurance written by the apostle John. "This then is how we know that we belong to the truth, and how we set our hearts at rest in his presence whenever our hearts condemn us. For God is greater than our hearts, and he knows everything" (1 John 3:19–20).

In other words, the reality and truth of who God is and the promises He has made are more significant than the doubts and misgivings that so frequently arise in the life of a believer. The antidote to this kind of self-condemnation and fear and mistrust is a solid, experiential grasp of what the Bible has to say.

Many believers ask this question concerning their faith in the same way Joseph's brothers asked whether his professions of forgiveness and reconciliation were real.

Hebrews 10 provides great encouragement for those who are struggling in this area of assurance and wrestle with doubts and fears.

The Path to Assurance

The writer of Hebrews says that Jesus Christ came to make an offering for sin (Hebrews 10:5) and to do God's will (v. 7). Then he writes in verse 10, "And by that will, we have been made holy through the sacrifice of the body of Jesus Christ once for all." Six points from Hebrews 10:5–17 will give you principles you can use for your own study and encouragement.

1. *All that God wants to accomplish, and all that we need for salvation, has been accomplished in the giving of His Son* (v. 10). The work of Jesus Christ is perfect. His sacrifice on the cross is in need of no contingency plan. It was a once-and-for-all sacrifice. God's will was expressed in the giving of His Son.

2. *Jesus has done all that needs to be done in relationship to sin* (v. 12). Jesus offered His one sacrifice for sin and then "sat down at the right hand of God." Human priests had to offer animal sacrifices "day after day" (v. 11), performing the same routines repeatedly because the blood of animals could not provide final forgiveness for sin.

When we understand and believe in Christ's full and final sacrifice for sin, we can sing with confidence, "We stand in grace," without adding, "At least, I hope we do," or "Well, we were in grace last week."

"No," the believer says, "there's no 'What if?' to this because Christ has done all in relationship to sin."

3. *Christ has done all that needs to be done in relationship to God* (v. 12). He sat down at the right hand of God, signifying acceptance of His sacrifice by the Father.

The great need for Christ's sacrifice lies not in our predicament but in God's wrath. If God were complacent toward sin, there would have been no need of a sacrifice.

But because God is so holy He cannot even *look* on sin, and because all of His wrath had been revealed against all of the unrighteousness and the wickedness of people, the great need was for the wrath of God to be propitiated, or satisfied. Christ's death satisfied God, so that He is free to forgive repentant sinners.

4. *Christ has done all that needs to be done in relationship to Satan* (v. 13). "Since that time he [Christ] waits for his enemies to be made his footstool." The Evil One is a defeated foe; he holds no terrors for us.

Satan was checkmated at Calvary. The Father, Son, and Holy Spirit are content for the time being to wait for the inevitable submission of the defeated foe.

5. *The Holy Spirit bears witness to what is true concerning the believer* (vv. 15–16). We have these truths on the highest of authorities. "The Holy Spirit also testifies to us about this" (v. 15).

How does the Spirit testify to us about the truth of Christ? By a voice in our ear? A feeling in the tummy? No—by the words of Scripture. The Spirit comes to confirm in our hearts and our spirits the reality of the finished work of Christ.

"I will put my laws in their hearts, and I will write them on their minds," God says (v. 16). When you become a Christian, God gives you a new heart, shaped perfectly for His law.

The result is that God's law is not irksome to the believer, for his heart has been changed. God makes a covenant with us and puts His law in our hearts.

One of the ways we know ourselves to be truly redeemed is that there is no conflict between our hearts and the requirements of holy living. Progress in Christian living is progress in a life of obedience to God's law.

Now this is not moralism. As we discussed in an earlier chapter, moralism says, "Try to be what you are not." Christianity says, "Come and be what you are." Moralism is like a car with all the bells and whistles but no engine, no source of power to make everything work.

6. *The Holy Spirit bears witness to what is true concerning God* (v.

17). "Their sins and lawless acts I will remember no more." When we come again to God with our old regrets and past confessions, He looks upon us in wonder and says, "You really do surprise Me. I can't remember anything about that at all."

Dear reader, do you see the foolishness of our "What if?" fears? If Christ has borne the penalty of our sins, and God does not even remember our past offenses, why are we so fearful?

If Joseph as a mere man could forgive his brothers so completely that they had nothing to fear, how much more can we rest in humble confidence in Christ. We can sing, "I need no other argument, I need no other plea; it is enough that Jesus died, and that He died for me."

The reason Joseph's brothers could not believe his forgiveness was full and final was that they could not believe themselves to be forgiven.

THE PLAN OF JOSEPH'S BROTHERS

Because of the fears Joseph's brothers harbored, they came up with another scheme (Genesis 50:15–17). They concocted a letter that Jacob had supposedly left behind when he died, in which he pled for Joseph to forgive his brothers.

You'll notice that the brothers did not take the letter to Joseph themselves. They sent a messenger with the letter, hoping to soften him up before they came and threw themselves down before him, saying, "We are your slaves" (v. 18).

After all these years of living in blessing because of Joseph, they reverted to their old conniving ways when their father was gone. Old habits die hard.

When Joseph got the concocted message from his brothers and then saw them lying on the ground before him offering to be his slaves, his emotions were deeply stirred. Let's notice two things about his reaction.

Joseph's Tears

Joseph cried when he heard his brothers' message (v. 17). He cried because he realized that his brothers had never truly believed him or accepted his forgiveness. The reality of it broke Joseph's heart.

It's interesting that their scheme didn't make Joseph indignant or stir him to anger or resentment. He was an amazing person. A lesser man might have become sick of the whole lot of them and decided it was time for revenge after all.

Joseph realized that the motives behind his efforts at reconciliation and his expressions of kindness toward his brothers and their families had been completely misunderstood and his sincerity doubted. This must have hurt him deeply.

Joseph's Theology

In his response to his brothers Joseph displayed more than tears. He also conveyed, once again, that when it came to the truth, he had his life wired correctly.

What was it over the years that enabled Joseph to resist temptation, endure hardship, keep his spirits up even when people let him down, and keep on going even when his circumstances were almost unbearable?

The answer was his theology—what he knew and believed about God. That was what allowed Joseph to look past his tears and speak to his brothers with clarity and compassion.

"Don't be afraid. Am I in the place of God? You intended to harm me, but God intended it for good to accomplish what is now being done, the saving of many lives. So then, don't be afraid. I will provide for you and your children" (vv. 19–21).

Notice, first of all, that Joseph had learned to leave the righting of one's wrongs to God. Grace and tenderness flowed from him as he reassured his brothers.

But Joseph didn't ignore or trivialize the offense. He knew what his brothers had done, and why. He spoke straightforwardly, calling a spade a spade. That was to be preferred to superficial smiles, nursed grievances, and repressed aggression. He was not about to assume a prerogative that wasn't his.

No matter how strongly we may want to exact vengeance, the way to overrule our corrupt hearts and keep our hands from evil is to consider afresh God's love and mercy toward us.

Paul addresses this issue in Romans 12:19. "Do not take revenge, my friends, but leave room for God's wrath, for it is written: 'It is mine to avenge; I will repay,' says the Lord." Our responsibility is to "overcome evil with good" (v. 21).

A second theological lesson Joseph had learned—as we have discussed before—was God's providence even in the face of man's malice. Throughout all the years of injustice, Joseph displayed a keen awareness of God's hand in a way that would ultimately be expressed in the theme verse for this book: "We know that in all things God works for the good of those who love him, who have been called according to his purpose" (Romans 8:28).

Joseph could look into the eyes of his brothers and say, "I know you planned to harm me. I know those people bought me so that they could make a profit from me. I know Potiphar's wife sent me to jail because she was jealous and spiteful and hateful. But through it all, I've learned to trust in God and depend upon His Word."

Here is a third theological lesson Joseph learned: It is right to repay evil not simply with kindness and forgiveness, but with practical affection. "He reassured [his brothers] and spoke kindly to them" (Genesis 50:21).

The text doesn't say that Joseph reassured his brothers *by* speaking kindly to them. Reassuring his brothers and speaking kindly to them were two different things. Joseph gave evidence to his loved ones of the good intentions of his heart by his *words* and his *deeds*, by his *promises* and his *performance*.

Does this story not remind you of the Prodigal Son (Luke 15:11–32)?

When he got out of the bathtub and looked at the robe and

the ring and the shoes, he knew they were the tokens of forgiveness. As he slipped them on he might have remarked, "I know my father loves me. He has not only told me, he has showed me."

We can say today, "I know my Father loves me. He *told* me in various ways through the prophets, and He *showed* me in the person of His Son." In Joseph's loving response to his brothers, we see a glimpse of God the Father's expression of love toward us.

The funeral of Jacob did not change Joseph's heart. His heart was the same after the funeral as it was when his father was still alive. Joseph was also a son of the heavenly Father. He bore the family likeness, being kind to his ungrateful and wicked brothers.

ℱACING DEATH, LEAVING A LEGACY

As we come to the last chapter in our study of this amazing, remarkable, godly man named Joseph, we can look back on a long and fascinating journey. The young man of seventeen we met in Genesis 37:2 is now an elderly 110 years of age. He has lived long enough to see his great-great-grandchildren.

After settling anew the issue of forgiveness with his brothers, Joseph "stayed in Egypt" (Genesis 50:22) and, indeed, died in Egypt. Notice the final statement in the book. "He was placed in a coffin in Egypt" (v. 26).

That may be the end of Genesis, but it's not the end of the story. The reference to Joseph's being placed in a coffin, coupled with the fact that he made his brothers swear to carry his bones back to Canaan, points toward the time when God would fulfill His word and bring His people Israel to their home in Canaan.

Joseph's coffin was an object lesson pointing subsequent generations toward that future event. Those generations recognized that the coffin was being kept for a reason greater than some morbid interest in bones. It was kept as a vital symbol of the provision of God in the past and the prospect of His glorious deliverance in the future.

JOSEPH STOOD THE TEST OF TIME

The least we can say about Joseph is that he stood the test of time. Anyone who can live a life of faithfulness to God for more than one hundred years is worthy of our admiration.

Joseph's Later Years

It is interesting that for all we know about Joseph, his final years are passed over in silence in Scripture. Verses 22–26 of Genesis 50 cover the last fifty or sixty years of his life. In that little phrase, "Joseph stayed in Egypt, along with all his father's family" (v. 22), many years are compressed—enough in themselves for an ordinary lifetime.

Compared to all that had happened to him as a lad and a young man, Joseph's latter years must have seemed dull. But even in those routine years, as his family grew, Joseph never allowed his heart to become fully "at home" in Egypt. He kept his focus on something larger than a comfortable retirement—he clung to the promises of God.

Keeping the Faith

There's a lesson for us here. It's one thing to have a vibrant and unwavering faith in those exciting and formative years when we're in the middle of the battle and engaging the challenges and difficulties of life. But it's quite another to live a life of steady obedience in the midst of everyday routines—and it is the routines of life that make up most of our days.

Certainly none of our lives can come close to equaling the dramatic events experienced by Joseph during the first half of his pilgrimage on Earth.

Most of us get up in the morning and begin an established routine. We do the same things over and over. Life can become a long slide into the retirement years. Just when we think we're getting somewhere, along comes a television advertiser spouting all kinds of numbers and scaring us to death about whether we'll have enough stored up to retire comfortably.

The question is: Are we going to buy into the mythology that we need to kill ourselves trying to "make it" for as many years as we can so that we can line the nest in which we plan to hibernate? If we believe this, our whole lives will become merely preparation for hibernation.

Planning to Quit

I want to give you a word of warning and a word of encouragement if you are beginning to think that way. I must ask you: What are you planning to do between the ages of sixty and one hundred ten? Are you going to sit on the skills and resources God has given you? Or are you going to use those treasures for His glory?

Joseph's horizons reached far beyond Egypt. He was looking ahead to the day God would redeem His people from Egypt. Joseph's responsibility was to ensure that his children and his children's children did not become comfortable in Egypt. He wanted his family to look ahead to the day when they would truly be settled in the Land of Promise.

Joseph wanted to make sure his people kept Canaan in mind. He did not want them to put down roots in Egyptian soil. He wanted his descendants to be ready to move when the call came from God to leave for the Promised Land. And Joseph wanted to make sure that they took his body with them as a testimony to his confidence in God's promises.

Keeping Our Bags Packed

We can be sure that during the last fifty or sixty years of his life, Joseph constantly reminded his family of their true home and of God's purpose for His people. His last words were surely an echo of the theme song of his life: "God will surely come to your aid and take you up out of this land to the land he promised on oath to Abraham, Isaac and Jacob" (v. 24).

When I was a boy, I took many journeys around our area of Scotland with my grandfather, and informally he taught me a great deal. Many of us have similar recollections, lessons we learned on our grandfather's knee or walking by his side.

It was probably just the same for Joseph's grandchildren. When they went to see Grandpa Joseph, he always told them the same things. He told them about their heritage and the Land of Promise their great-grandfather Jacob had left. And he told them that someday their family would return to their true home in Canaan.

Grandpa Joseph would tell his grandchildren, "You know, we're going to go back to Canaan one day. God is going to bring us back. Don't start liking Egypt too much or get too involved here, because we're going somewhere else."

This isn't just conjecture. Of all the things the writer of Hebrews could have recorded about Joseph, he chose this recollection: "By faith Joseph, when his end was near, spoke about the exodus of the Israelites from Egypt and gave instructions about his bones" (Hebrews 11:22).

Isn't that interesting? Why did the writer choose to report this fact about Joseph? Because it was so incredibly significant.

Joseph bore an Egyptian title, married an Egyptian wife, and enjoyed the Egyptian lifestyle, yet he never bought the whole package. He wasn't content just to live out his retirement years in comfort, with his grandchildren playing at his feet. He kept his eyes on a much bigger prize. He stood the test of time.

Think how amazing Joseph's commitment was. He was living in the most advanced civilization of his day. He was deeply involved in the political, social, and economic structure of Egypt. Next to Pharaoh, he was the most recognized man in the country.

And yet when Joseph gathered his children and grandchildren and great-grandchildren around him, he reminded them, "Our security is not in my position. Our hope for the future is not tied to things in Egypt. God has helped us in the past, and all of our hope is in Him. We are going to return to the Land of Promise someday. And I want you to take my bones with you."

As in the words of Romans 12:1–2, Joseph continually offered himself as a living sacrifice to God, refusing to "conform [himself] . . . to the pattern of this world."

Living as a Stranger

Is this not one of our greatest challenges: to stand the test of time and stay the course in the Christian life?

J. B. Phillips paraphrases Romans 12:2 in this way: "Don't let the world around you squeeze you into its own [mold]." Just because everybody else is putting down deep roots in this world and lining the retirement nest doesn't mean that's what we are supposed to do.

Joseph's great challenge was to have an Egyptian title, marry an Egyptian wife, and live in the Egyptian culture while keeping his focus on God's agenda. Our challenge is the same today. The only difference is that the cultures have different names.

It takes a firm commitment to live in this world and yet keep reminding our children and grandchildren, "This world is not where it's at."

Some of us can't say this because everything we're doing with our time, talents, and money says to our kids, "This world *is* it. This is all there is. That's why I'm working all the time and can't come home. That's why I can only take two days of vacation. That's why I'm sorry I wasn't at your ball game. That's why I won't be at my grandchild's concert."

Colossians 3:1–2 tells us, "Since, then, you have been raised with Christ, set your hearts on things above, where Christ is seated at the right hand of God. Set your minds on things above, not on earthly things." Don't get too embroiled in this world. Don't get weighed down by the earthbound stuff.

Peter says we are "aliens and strangers" in this world (1 Peter 2:11). There are several ways we can go about this business of living as aliens and strangers.

We could buy ourselves togas and sandals, put flowers in our hair, and drop out of society, condemning all those dull people who wear business suits and go to work every day. Or we could do something else to mark ourselves as eccentric.

But the far harder thing is to drive the same kind of car, wear the same kind of clothes, shop in the same stores, and go to the same schools as the people around us and yet live in a way that marks us, not as weird, but as distinctively belonging to Jesus Christ.

From one perspective the future of the church in the United States is directly related to how well we do this. Paul wrote to the Philippians, "But our citizenship is in heaven. And we eagerly await a savior from there, the Lord Jesus Christ" (Philippians 3:20). To live this way marked Paul and the Philippians as strange.

All those years before, Joseph was living as a stranger in the world as represented in Egypt. How strange are we prepared to become as we seek to stand the test of time?

JOSEPH FACED THE FINAL CURTAIN

Like his father Jacob before him (Genesis 46:30), Joseph faced the prospect of his death with striking realism. "I am about to die," he told his brothers (50:24).

This is remarkable because dying men and women are often unwilling to believe that which is apparent to everybody else. But with Joseph there was no terror in the face of death, nor grasping at shadows or clutching at vain things.

He knew he was close to death, but the important thing to him was not his own demise, but communicating to his family a strong assurance: "God will surely come to your aid and take you up out of this land to the land he promised" (v. 24).

As I think about the way Joseph faced the final curtain of death, my mind goes back to 1976 and a hospice on the outskirts of Edinburgh. I went there to visit a lady who, along with her husband, had been a missionary in China for a large part of her life.

She had piercing blue eyes and gray hair, which she always kept long, though always tied up. This dear woman had terminal cancer, and in the routine of my responsibilities as the assistant minister in the church, I went to visit her.

As I spoke with her on this particular afternoon, she was very lucid. I took her hand and she squeezed mine. Then she asked me about my wife and the prayer meeting that had taken place the previous evening. She asked me about a whole variety of things in relationship to the church.

Then we read the Scriptures and prayed together, and I came back to the center of Edinburgh to say that I felt this woman was rallying a little bit. The person to whom I was speaking let me finish my sentence and then informed me that the woman had passed away between the time I left her an hour earlier and the time I arrived back at the office. All of her dying concerns had to do with everybody except herself. There was no paranoia or undue fearfulness in the face of imminent death.

That's what we find in Joseph. He encouraged those who would be left behind with a strong reminder of the covenant promise of God. He even repeated his assurance in verse 25. Joseph's dying concern was reiterating the promise God had made to Abraham, Isaac, and Jacob.

We find Joseph on his deathbed saying, "I want you to understand that God gave His promise to Abraham, He affirmed it to Isaac, and He reaffirmed it to my father, Jacob. God's promise is not in question. I am so sure He will fulfill it that I want you to carry my bones with you when you leave this place" (see vv. 24–25).

JOSEPH CROSSED THE GREAT DIVIDE

After affirming God's promise, Joseph died at the age of 110 (v. 26). His long pilgrimage was over.

A Memorial of God's Promise

His body was embalmed and placed in a coffin. Why? Because the coffin itself would be a memorial affirming the fact that God's promise to take His people back to the Promised Land was as certain as any promise God had ever made.

Joseph didn't want his bones to be buried permanently in Egypt. When the Israelites got ready to leave, he wanted to go with them. Perhaps he sensed that difficult days were ahead for this people Israel when they grew in number and strength as refugees in a hostile environment.

And, indeed, difficult days did come. A new king who didn't know Joseph came to power in Egypt, and he decided it was time to enslave the Israelites because they had become too strong (see Exodus 1:8–14).

"God Will Surely Come to Your Aid"

So, as unusual as it may seem to us, Joseph's coffin spoke of God's provision in the past and His promise for the future.

For us, it is not a coffin that speaks of God's promised redemption, but a cave. An *empty* cave, the burial place of Jesus Christ.

What is the strength of our conviction that we can stand the test of time and face death with faith and confidence? It is because Jesus lives that we can face tomorrow. It is because Jesus lives that all fear is gone. It is because Jesus holds the future in His hands that we may face death calmly. It is because Jesus lives that we will live also (see John 14:19).

The thing that is so precious to me as I look at the death of Joseph is his parting word, "God will surely come to your aid." Isn't that the message of the Bible?

Joseph did not know the totality of what those words meant, but he knew they were true. He couldn't see ahead to the birth of Moses and God's protection of the deliverer as a baby stashed among the reeds (Exodus 2:1–10). Joseph couldn't know that God would come to His people's aid through Moses (Exodus 3–13).

But as the people walked through the Red Sea on dry ground and saw the pursuing Egyptians drowned (Exodus 14), they could say, "God surely has come to our aid. This is what our ancestor Joseph was telling us about. This is the promise he wanted us never to forget."

God's people were living under God's hand. In the wilderness wanderings, when the Israelites were thirsty and hungry, they had spring water better than the best bottled water you can buy (Exodus 17). And they had manna every morning (Exodus 16). God came to their aid.

When it came time for the nation to enter Canaan, God provided a leader named Joshua (Deuteronomy 32:44; Joshua 1:1–9). God came to their aid again. And then, through the line of the kings, the prophets stood on tiptoe, looking ahead and saying, "God will surely come to our aid." Micah the prophet said, "God will come to our aid through a Child born in Bethlehem" (see Micah 5:2).

Then came the moment when the angel told another Joseph not to fear taking Mary as his wife, because the Baby within her was God in the flesh, the Messiah (Matthew 1:18–24). God had surely come to the aid of His people.

The great message of the Bible is that God comes to the aid of the helpless and the hopeless and the needy, but sets His face against the aid of the arrogant, the self-assertive, and those who face the final curtain declaring, "I did it my way."

Those who come to Christ saying, "Nothing in my hand I bring, simply to Your cross I cling," find Him coming to their aid. This message that gives us eternal hope was first delivered by Joseph as he crossed the great divide.

JOSEPH LEFT A GREAT LEGACY

Joseph bequeathed to his posterity a priceless heritage of faith and an ironclad trust in God's promises.

Joseph Inherited a Legacy

Joseph was also the recipient of such a heritage. Nowhere does the Bible say that God appeared to Joseph in any direct way, or that Joseph received a message from God at the hands of an angel.

But Joseph did not acquire his faith in a vacuum. Somehow in those seventeen years Joseph had at home, even amid all of Jacob's intrigues and jealousies and mistakes, the patriarch must have instilled in his son Joseph great and magnificent truths about God.

Joseph had no written word from God, and we have no record that he ever received an audible word from God. He had only the words of his father, Jacob, speaking of the truth of God as he himself had learned it from his father, Isaac, and his grandfather, Abraham. This legacy was sufficient ground for Joseph's faith and for his sure confidence in God's promises.

Therefore, when Joseph spoke of God's faithfulness from his deathbed, he was passing on what Abraham had passed on to Isaac, and what Isaac had passed on to Jacob. Joseph passed on a wonderful legacy.

The Legacy We Leave

What legacy are we passing on to our children and grand-children? We have a tremendous advantage over the patriarchs because we have "the word of the prophets made more certain" (2 Peter 1:19).

We don't have to rely on or seek a visitation of angels, nor do we need to rely on dramatic experiences that are beyond the Scriptures. We find ourselves affirming the words of John Calvin when he says, "Unless the hearing of the Word of God is sufficient for our faith, we don't deserve that God should condescend to deal with us."

You and I will leave some kind of legacy to our posterity. And because we have all the word from God we will ever need, we can bequeath to our descendants the truth of God in all of its fullness.

Paul understood he would leave a legacy to those who had been under his care. In 1 Corinthians 15:3–5 he said, "What I received I passed on to you as of first importance: that Christ died for our sins according to the Scriptures, that he was buried, that he was raised on the third day according to the Scriptures, and that he appeared to Peter, and then to the Twelve."

Paul's legacy was the truth of Scripture, the reality of Christ's redemption in fulfillment of God's Word. He was careful to pass this treasure on to his spiritual son, Timothy, telling him, "What you heard from me, keep as the pattern of sound teaching, with faith and love in Christ Jesus. Guard the good deposit that was entrusted to you—guard it with the help of the Holy Spirit who lives in us" (2 Timothy 1:13–14).

Peter had the same goal. He wrote to the believers scattered among the regions of the world, saying, "I will always remind you of these things, even though you know them and are firmly established in the truth you now have. I think it is right to refresh your memory as long as I live in the tent of this body. . . . I will make every effort to see that after my departure you will always be able to remember these things" (2 Peter 1:12–13, 15).

Joseph did the same thing. He kept reminding his generation, and future generations, of God's sure promises. In doing so, he left us a legacy that is wonderful.

Joseph left us a record of steadfast faith in the face of extreme trial. He left us a graphic picture of forgiveness in response to bitter jealousy. He left us a wonderful testimony of generosity and kindness as repayment for cruel neglect.

In closing we must ask, What kind of legacy will *we* leave? What pictures of faith, perseverance, and Christlikeness will our children and grandchildren be able to call to mind concerning us? In what ways are we preparing the next generation for the journey ahead of them?

It is a sobering question. Let us take courage from the fact

that we serve a wonderful, merciful, holy, and changeless God.
He holds all of creation in His hand and moves all in accordance with His sovereign purposes.

If I had been asked to choose funeral hymns for Joseph I
would have included these.

> Under the shadow of Thy throne
> Thy saints have dwelt secure;
> Sufficient is Thine arm alone,
> And our defense is sure.

Joseph would have affirmed those words from Isaac Watts
and would have recognized the helpfulness of John Wesley's
hymn:

> Commit thy ways to Him
> Thy works into His hands;
> And rest in His unchanging Word
> Who heaven and earth commands.

> Through waves and clouds and storms
> His power will clear thy way;
> Wait thou His time; the darkest night
> Shall end in brightest day.

> Leave to His sovereign sway
> To choose and to command;
> So shalt thou, wondering, own His way
> How wise, how strong His hand.

More Excellent Reading by Alistair Begg

What Angels Wish They Knew

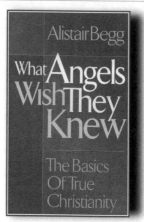

In an age that grants plausibility to every idea and certainty to none - what can you believe?

If you have ever wandered around a mall, browsed a bookstore, or explored the Internet, you've seen the evidence: We live in a culture desperately searching for meaning. Like the ancient Greeks, we are haunted by questions. Where did this world come from? Why am I here? As individuals and as a society, we are restless, longing for something, or someone, to believe in.

There are perhaps millions of potential answers- but only one truth that wholly explains, resolves, and offers hope for the plight of man. Within these pages, author Alister Begg explores "these things" more fully, offering fresh insights into the mystery and power of the gospel account and presenting a convincing argument to all those seeking answers to the meaning of life.

ISBN: 0-8024-1708-6, Paperback

MOODY
The Name You Can Trust
1-800-678-8812 www.MoodyPress.org

Made for His Pleasure

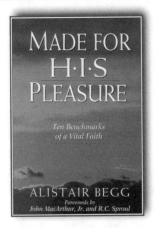

- The Benchmarks of a Vital Faith -

The prayer that pleases God is larger than ourselves. It focuses on the glory of God and remembers the the needs of others. The life that is truly fulfilling gives back to God the talents and abilities He has given us to be used for His glory.

Alistair Begg applies these principles to ten areas of our lives and challenges us to experience our Father's pleasure as we glorify Him.

"This book from the pen of Alistair Begg is a chronicle of his own spiritual pilgrimage. It reads as a spiritual road map, a trustworthy guide to vital faith and life."
R.C. Sproul

ISBN: 0-8024-7138-2, Hardcover

MOODY
The Name You Can Trust
1-800-678-8812 www.MoodyPress.org